PRAISE FOR *MAX POTENTIAL*

"You get one life to do everything you've dreamed of and to make a difference in the world. Aaron Ammar will get you excited about that potential and get you started on the right path to the life you really want."

–RYAN ALLIS, Chairman of Hive Global

"*Max Potential* teaches you how to go after what you want with everything you have, while keeping all areas of your life in balance. There's no limit to what you can achieve when you follow Aaron's advice and keep after your goals, day after day."

–KURT RATHMANN, CEO & Founder of ScaleFactor, Inc.

"*Max Potential* is thought-provoking, insightful, and rich with ideas to help millennials better understand how to be intentional in their journey to achieve happiness and fulfillment. Aaron's real-life storytelling style is engaging and the common-sense principles he draws on can be used the minute you put the book down."

–JOHN HAHN, Founder and CEO of EPIC Brokers and Consultants

"The world needs more of what Aaron Ammar has to offer! *Max Potential* is a must-read for students, recent grads, and anyone who just wants more from life."

–HEATHER NORRIS, Dean of Appalachian State University Walker College of Business

AARON AMMAR

FOREWORD BY JEFF SATURDAY

MAX

ON HAPPINESS, FULFILLMENT, AND BEING
BETTER THAN YOU WERE YESTERDAY

POTENTIAL

Published by Always Smilin Press
West Hartford, CT
http://www.alwayssmilin.com

Cataloging-in-Publication data is available.

Print ISBN: 978-1-7329634-0-5

Cover and book design by Brian Phillips Design

Printed in the United States of America
19 20 21 22 23 24   8 7 6 5 4 3 2 1

ALWAYS SMILIN

FOREWORD

FOR MANY YEARS, I played professional football, and these days I talk about it for a living.

On the weekends during the NFL season, I watch the games being played, and when I go into work on Monday, I analyze them. I often speak to schools or groups about what I've learned through these years of experience on topics ranging from perseverance and hard work to leadership and excellence. And it's not uncommon to be approached by someone looking for a personal mentor.

I keep my time tightly scheduled, preferring to stay busy with my family and work. There's very little downtime in between it all. So when a coworker at ESPN approached me and asked if I would meet up with her boyfriend who was looking for someone to help him grow in his faith, I hesitated slightly. I only had so much to give, and I wasn't sure I had more in me.

But I agreed and met up with Aaron for dinner one night at a little restaurant in West Hartford, Connecticut. I remember clearly that he walked in with this massive smile on his face. We sat outside, grabbed some food and a few beers, and—suddenly—a few hours had passed.

We talked like old friends, and I was struck by the vulnerability he showed. At the same time, he carried that vulnerability lightly, always with a smile or a positive spin. Immediately, I could tell that this guy was who he was. There was no hiding it, no changing it.

And you know what? That authentic combination of vulnerability and positivity is infectious.

Over time, our friendship grew. I realized that what I expected to be a more one-sided mentorship, with me doling out advice to a younger guy, turned out to be a real exchange of ideas. I pushed him on things, sure, challenging his ideas where we disagreed. And every time I did, he took that perspective, thought about it for several days, and put his heart firmly behind what he believed. Sometimes that meant changing his mind, and other times it meant strengthening his current belief.

When we did disagree, he remained completely amiable. Not once have I seen him become combative about his ideas. Thoughtful? Definitely. Defensive? Never.

At a time when watching the news can induce a headache, when everyone seems to be in opposition to someone or something else, it's rare to see someone respond to a differing opinion with grace. In my conversations with Aaron, I recognized that sometimes it's not about the idea at all—it's about how we respond to it. It's about using differences or disagreements to grow or push us toward something better.

And when one of my own ideas or suggestions took hold with Aaron, he didn't just respond with politeness. Rather, he ran 100 miles an hour in the direction of that idea with so much positivity and drive that I found myself wanting to be better.

One of the most challenging aspects of helping someone or lifting them up is that doing so forces you to see the hypocrisy in yourself. It's one thing to talk the talk; it's another thing to walk the walk. And there were times when I saw Aaron taking my advice better than I had.

In the end, the guy I expected to mentor turned out to shape me more than I could have known at our first meeting. I had no idea how he'd push me to be better through his example and the sheer force of his positivity. I laugh to think of my initial hesitation now. What I would have missed out on if I'd said no.

If you spend any time with Aaron, if you hear him speak or read his words, you'll feel that forceful positivity. Whether you're seeking it out or not, his drive and optimism and compassion will rub off on you. As I said, it's *infectious*.

So make the time. Read his words with an open heart and disagree with grace. Run 100 miles an hour toward the ideas that inspire you. And by all means, be the person who approaches life with a massive smile. You'll be glad you did.

———

JEFF SATURDAY
Super Bowl Champion, Indianapolis Colts Ring of Honor Member,
Six-Time Pro Bowler, Four-Time All Pro, and NFL ESPN Analyst

INTRODUCTION

MORNINGS ARE A SPECIAL TIME FOR ME. I've been a morning person for as long as I can remember, often waking up my brothers and sister when we were kids to go play outside or my parents on Christmas morning. These days, it's my wife, to go on a run.

One morning, while my family was vacationing in the mountains of North Carolina, I decided to wake them all up to look at the colorful sunrise. I had a pillow thrown at my head.

I've learned over the years that my appreciation for early mornings is not shared by all. It only took a few more pillows being pelted at my head to figure that one out. So while I may not wake up others as often these days, it doesn't stop me from being the upbeat, happy morning person that I am.

I'm just a little quieter about it than I used to be.

A few years ago, I woke up at my usual time of 5 a.m., took my dog on a walk, worked out, and thought to myself, *What next?* Without any other pressing things to do that morning, I decided to head into work early.

It should come as no surprise that I'm usually the first one in the office. Most mornings, I'll walk into our company's open floor plan space, turn on all the lights, grab a cup of coffee, and settle into my day's work.

As colleagues start to file in, we'll chat, quietly jam to some music, maybe play the news on the TV that overlooks our desks. Whatever we need to get the energy up among our small group.

On this particular morning, there was a thick snow on the ground. Moving from Houston, Texas, to Hartford, Connecticut, was a rude awakening in terms of dealing with cold weather, but I had come to appreciate the snow. (Finally buying a real winter coat didn't hurt either.) It may be a pain to shovel and definitely took some getting used to, but there's nothing like a fresh snowfall to make you appreciate life's treasures.

From inside the office, I can see a river through the large open windows, but I had never stepped outside to intentionally walk along it. Getting out of the car that day, I decided this would be the time to change that. So I walked through the parking lot and around the outside of our building to the river that runs behind it. The snow crunched under my boots, and the sun was just peeking over the horizon. There were no other people walking along the narrow trail. The only noise I could hear was a faint rumble from traffic on nearby streets.

When I got closer to the water, I noticed that ice was starting to form around the banks. The water was moving so slowly, too. The tree branches were low and heavy with snow. Everything was incredibly still.

And that's when the analogy that life is like a river came to me.

Oh, you've heard that one before? Okay then, but have you heard that life is *most* like the Farmington River just outside of Hartford?

It struck me that day that I could learn a thing or two from that river. The first lesson being stillness.

You see, over a decade ago, I made a decision about my life. I was going to wake up each morning better than I was the day before.

In the time between making that decision and this walk along the river, I would do things like park a little farther away at the grocery store to boost my health. I'd make it a goal to pay someone a compliment. I'd read a new book or talk to a friend about a Bible passage.

I would set my alarm for a few minutes earlier than normal to do some push-ups. I'd take a few deep breaths and give a driver the benefit of the doubt after being cut off. I'd grab coffee with a mentor or a friend. I might make a point to turn off the TV for an entire week. One day, I even decided to walk around West Hartford wishing everyone I saw Merry Christmas and Happy Holidays.

As you might be able to tell, there wasn't much of a pattern to it. I knew that over time all these actions would add up to a stronger, kinder, wiser person. What I didn't know was what that person would be able to do. What kind of impact could my future self really have? What did I want to be better for?

Which leads us back to stillness. I needed it in my life. I needed it to find gratitude and appreciation for all of the people and opportunities in my life. I needed it to be able to process all of the things I was doing to improve myself. And I needed it to get to know myself.

I also came to realize that stillness and gratitude make up a two-way street. With stillness, you are able to think more clearly about your life and find appreciation for what you have. Likewise, one of the quickest ways to calm your mind, to quiet the doubts and to-do lists and constant stream of information, is to think about what you are grateful for.

Ask yourself, what is one good thing that happened today? What am I most looking forward to this week? What am I thankful for in my life? When you refocus your thoughts on the positive aspects of your life, you will be amazed by how quickly you will find calm.

This book is all about making yourself better one day at a time and not settling for less than your full potential. But before I start sharing tips and tricks for how to do that, let me pause and share one of the most important lessons I've learned. Find a source of stillness in your life. Allow yourself time and quiet to focus, and use gratitude to get into the right state of mind. Find a reason to slow down and evaluate the choices you make. After all, happiness is found in the journey, not the destination.

For me, walks along the Farmington River of Life became a routine. I began to crave that time because I was able to see the impact that my choices were having. Some bigger themes started to come into focus. I realized that all of the actions I took could be classified into 5 buckets, which we'll go through soon. And after all that, I created my own mission statement for my life.

So besides being a naturally happy morning person, what qualifies me to give advice and share my perspective about all of this?

The truth: not *that* much. I don't pretend to have all the answers. But I have been paying close attention to cultivating my own happiness with intention over the last decade and have helped many of the people in my network do the same.

I want to share what I've discovered with you. I believe that the people we surround ourselves with can have an enormous impact on our lives, and I want to be there as a positive force for you. I want this book to radiate positive vibes when you pick it up. I want to be a friend and ally on your own journey toward your own version of happiness. Let's be clear. My happiness and yours won't look alike. But together we'll move day by day toward the people we want to be.

MORE ABOUT ME

Before we go any further, let me share a little bit about myself. Since high school, I have always held at least two jobs: my day job and a side business. When I was in high school, my day job was as a student, while my side job was founding a pressure washing company in Houston. We did several hundred jobs over many years, and I learned a huge amount about running a business. More than that, I figured out the value of my time.

When I went to college, I could have spent all of my time at bars (and I did do that a fair amount), but joining entrepreneurship groups and working on my pressure washing business, amongst other business ventures, taught me that whatever job I took after graduation didn't need to be my only source of income. Or fulfillment. If I prioritized my time wisely, I could have more. I could be in charge of my own destiny.

I'd be remiss if I didn't give credit where credit is due. The entrepreneurial seed was planted by my parents, who raised my two brothers, my sister, and me to have strong work ethics. I can still hear my dad's voice when he told me, "Make your money work for you. Don't work for your money."

I realize now that I'm starting my own family with my wife Joslyn how much that phrase was less about money and more about time. Making sure I have enough of it to spend with the people who matter most. But even before I fully understood the importance of his words, I kept them front and center after graduating.

My first job out of college was through an underwriting professional development program that only a small group of graduates nationwide were chosen to be a part of. I worked hard in college, earning a double major in Finance & Banking and Risk Management & Insurance, to find an opportunity like this. It was an incredible learning experience, but a few months after starting, I felt the itch for another job, or rather an investment opportunity. This time, I founded a company with some friends to buy residential real estate properties. We started off with a couple houses around our alma mater in North Carolina that we rented to college students, and these days we've expanded to new cities and continue to rent out various single-family homes.

Two years ago, after working with the leadership of a large insurance company, I took the biggest leap in my career so far, becoming a founding partner at a company that insures businesses in the sharing and on-demand economy. Think about your favorite rideshare company, or the last place you stayed on vacation. How do you insure something like that? It was a question many people hadn't stopped to fully consider when we started. It's a new frontier, and it's fascinating.

It's not every day that insurance companies function like start-ups, but this one does. We're a small team, and each of us has a big impact on the company's growth. Every day, I find myself surrounded by smart, like-minded people and get to do something I find truly exciting.

I've been blessed in my career, and I've also done a lot of work to land where I am today. I bring it up because our professional lives are often held up as our greatest potential source of fulfillment. For me, it has had a big impact on my happiness, and I hope that my ability to balance multiple professional pursuits at once shows you a few things: First, that you aren't limited to a line on a resume and, second, that when you're aware of how you spend your time, you can allocate it to the things that matter most. For me, relationships are what matter most.

RELATIONSHIPS ARE EVERYTHING

I'm going to talk a lot about relationships over the course of this book (get ready!) because the role that I have taken up in so many of my relationships is another key factor that led me to write this book, more so than my professional experience.

Being there for others has always come natural to me. And I truly enjoy it. While I have a great support system, I have also assumed that role for many other people over the years, starting with my family. While my parents were always there for us, being the oldest of four meant that being a sounding board for my two brothers and sister was par for the course. And as we've grown into adults and their decisions have become bigger, being that sounding board has become even more rewarding.

When my sister, Hanna, ran her very first half-marathon this year, I was there to cheer her on when she didn't want to go on a training run or when she got down on herself. There were times when she would call me and talk about backing out of the race, and my job as her big brother was to be there with a huge dose of encouragement. When she crossed the finish line and achieved one of her long-standing goals, I felt enormous pride. And, you know what, it felt great to have played a small role in her journey.

I felt a similar joy when I helped my brother Ramsey out. Several years ago, he was trying to decide where to go to law school. He was just starting his applications and studying for the LSAT, but he seemed particularly overwhelmed with the process. So I invited him to stay with me in North Carolina, where I was living at the time, to focus on his applications for as long as he needed. I thought the change of scenery and lack of distractions may help him tackle everything he had coming up. On top of that, I was pretty stoked to live with my brother again.

One night, a few months after he moved in, we grabbed some food and sat down on the couch. He had bought a book with a list of the 300 top law schools in the United States and wanted my help to narrow it down. Before we started, I asked him why he wanted to go to law school. He looked confused, like I hadn't been listening to him the whole time he'd been there. The truth was that I wanted to dig a little deeper. Maybe doing so would help guide his choice.

"I want to make an impact," he said, with the tone of voice that implied he'd already said this about a million times.

"Okay, what else?" I said.

"I want to be financially secure."

"Great. What else?"

"I want to live in a cool new city with access to the outdoors. Meet new people."

"Which of these schools are going to help you do those things?"

That third answer, living in a vibrant new city, ended up being a big sticking point for him. He realized that, while lots of these schools could help him find a secure, meaningful job, only a handful would put him in an environment he truly enjoyed, where he could live in a dynamic city, spend time outdoors, and get to know some like-minded people.

We still talk about this conversation today, about how it was a light-bulb moment that helped him wade through the Princeton Review rankings and graduate hiring statistics to ultimately decide that the University of Denver was his top choice. He knew deep down what would make him happy. He just needed to reconnect with it.

A few years later, something similar happened with my youngest brother, Zak. He had graduated with his undergraduate degree a few months before and started working in sales. It didn't take long for Zak to realize that this kind of job wasn't going to work long-term. Unlike for our brother Ramsey, graduate school had yet to surface as a consideration for Zak. After a while, however, he found himself wanting more.

For the first time, he felt like he didn't have a clear path forward. And I felt very humbled by the fact that, at this difficult crossroads, he called me. Over the course of a few long-distance conversations, it became clear that most of his frustration with his job came from its limited scope. He wanted to be involved in all aspects of the business.

"Starting my own company," he said one day. "That's what I should be doing."

"I think you'd be great at that, Z," I said. "Do you have any business ideas right now? Would you feel ready to start something?"

At 22, he didn't know what kind of business he would start or how he would do it. He just knew that he had the drive for it. After a few months of mulling it over and getting comfortable with the idea, he decided to go back to school to study business and entrepreneurship.

That's how my involvement in Zak's professional world went. He'd come to me for support as he faced the next leap forward in his journey—where to go to school, what kind of business to start, how to structure the company. I'd talk him through those decisions, and he'd keep moving forward. Today, I'm on the board of his company, Vixster, and have watched him accomplish so many of his goals.

At their core, the decisions that Zak and Ramsey faced when they asked for my help were surprisingly similar. They both boiled down to where to go to grad school. But together they taught me how two seemingly similar decisions can be handled so differently. And these were two people from the same family, no less.

And what they needed from me was drastically different, too.

Shortly after Zak went off to business school, I enrolled in Jairek Robbins' Performance Coach University. I loved helping my siblings figure out their professional paths, and I wanted to put my natural inclination to help people to use with people outside of my immediate sphere. For months, my group studied how to bring out the best performances from people who were far more diverse than my immediate family.

We participated in webinars a few nights a week, in addition to doing a *lot* of required reading. We studied psychology and neuroscience. It felt like I was back in college, prepping for an upcoming exam, only this was more intense than any normal exam. And, on top of learning a huge amount, I truly enjoyed it.

In order to complete my training, I needed to record coaching sessions with two people and present them to the group. It was nerve-wracking to say the least, but in the end it reaffirmed what I had believed all along—that I could help people be the best they could be. On top of that, I had learned so many new skills that would help me do just that.

Shortly after completing the course, I got a phone call from a buddy of mine named John. He's a savvy businessman and great friend, but he was bothered and needed someone to talk to. A few years before, John had started a company with a business partner. Suddenly, his business partner wanted out.

John had been the figurehead of the company, driving company culture and vision. His partner, on the other hand, executed more of the financial aspects of the company. As business partners, they complemented each other nicely. Not only that, his partner had been the only other person John felt comfortable confiding in, especially since he was so involved in the operations of the company.

And so, in the blink of an eye, my friend was faced with a choice: keep leading the company alone, restructure the existing team, or bring someone else on board. He wasn't sure he could carry the load on his own or what that would look like, but he was still as passionate about his company as he was on day one. Someone I had always known to be confident and decisive was at a major crossroads in his career, looking not only for advice and perspective about how to proceed but also for emotional support. He was hurt.

We spoke on the phone for a few hours, and I mostly listened, asking some questions here and there. I knew that the stakes were high for John, and I didn't want to rush in with my own thoughts. So we talked through his options. We talked about the emotional impact. And we talked about the opportunities the situation presented. It wasn't a position he wanted to be in, but could he take the company somewhere new as a result? Was there a silver lining?

The silver lining turned out to be that he had some phenomenal employees working with him. Without his partner in the picture, he had a greater opportunity to get to know and empower them, and because of that, he decided to take things slow. Over the next few months, he found a circle of trusted employees that he could rely on to take on some of the responsibilities of his former partner. He restructured the executive team to reflect those changes and, in the process, felt a deeper connection to his work and the team around him.

John has a great mind for business, so I don't take credit for the decisions he made. But it sure felt good to be able to support him in that time of need and share a different perspective. To help shift his mindset from upset and betrayed to feeling a sense of opportunity and optimism. If there's a common thread through these experiences, it's that each person had the answers inside of them. All I did was help them shift their mindsets so that they could think more clearly and find those answers for themselves. Since then, the company has significantly multiplied in size and is one of the fastest growing companies in its region.

There's one more experience I'd like to share that doesn't necessarily fit the same mold. It's one of my most meaningful memories, and it shows the power we all have to shift the mindsets of others. Sometimes without even realizing it.

Living in Connecticut with my biological brothers and sister across the country, I guess you could say I missed having my family around me. I recognized how lucky I was to have such a tight-knit family, so I wanted to pay it forward and be there in the same way for someone else. I decided to join Big Brothers Big Sisters as a volunteer.

It took my Little Brother a while to trust that I wasn't just there to put community service hours on my resume. We'd go out and play basketball or go bowling. I'd ask him about school and homework. He'd mostly shrug off my questions. I tried to find activities for us to do together. Eventually, after a camping trip with their family, he came to trust that I was there for the right reasons and started opening up little by little.

One day, while we were driving to back to his house after we grabbed dinner, I asked him, "Buddy, what are you learning?"

"What do you mean? In school?" he asked.

"In school, in life, wherever," I said, smiling back him.

He thought for a second. It wasn't the first time I'd asked him this question. I always loved hearing what he liked learning about in school or what he picked up on from our own conversations.

"Well," he said, "you've been teaching me how to smile more."

I was floored. I do a lot of smiling, that's true. But getting him to smile more or be a happier kid wasn't my goal. My goal was to be there for him in whatever brotherly capacity he needed me and to be a positive example of my own family values. That he learned to smile more and find happiness around him more easily didn't come from anything I said. It just came from being myself, the naturally upbeat morning person who walks through West Hartford wishing people Merry Christmas for the heck of it. It's a moment that will stick with me for the rest of my life as a reminder of the power of the examples we set for each other.

So as we go through the rest of this book together, you can trust that I am walking the walk for everything that I share with you. I am living this philosophy each day and have been slowly sharing it with the people around me, whether through outright conversations about fulfillment or through simply setting the example.

As I write this, my wife Joslyn is pregnant with our first child. Finding out that we were expecting was one of the happiest days of my life, compared only to the day we got married. We had a little party to reveal the baby's gender, and I couldn't believe it when we popped the balloon we held and were covered in blue confetti. I was ecstatic.

But each day of the pregnancy makes it feel more and more real. And I've become more and more aware of how much my time will mean once our little guy arrives.

There's a lot of pressure to make sure that I provide a comfortable life for our son, and a great deal of that pressure comes from myself. Conventional wisdom says that dads like me should start putting in longer hours at the office, angling for a promotion or a raise. But to me, being a provider and being a dad also means being there for my son. Working smarter, not longer hours. Instilling the same principles in him that my dad did in me. Teaching him to smile by example. Helping him to understand who he is and where he'll fit in the world. Helping him be the best he can be.

With that kind of inspiration, I feel like the lessons and perspective

I'll share in this book are bursting out of me. But while I can't wait to pass this wisdom to him, there's an even more urgent need for the content. There's a reason you picked up this book. You want a change. And you're not alone.

LET'S TALK ABOUT YOU

I adopted the phrase "Be better than you were yesterday" as my personal motto around the time I was entering the workforce. I wanted to be sure that I found fulfillment in my life and didn't let my work ethic drive me to 90+ hour work weeks for the rest of my life.

I've heard from others who moved to a new city or started a new job and, after a few months, found themselves thinking, *Is this all?*

Holy smokes, is this what life is going to be like for me?

Shouldn't I be enjoying myself more?

Shouldn't I feel more fulfilled by the work I'm doing?

A recent LinkedIn survey found that 72%[1] of young professionals between 25 and 33 have experienced a quarter-life crisis. Can you believe that? We're a generation of worriers!

It seems that as Millenials, we've been handed down long-standing definitions of happiness—a steady job, a family, homeownership, financial security, and so on. Unfortunately, these definitions don't ring true for all people and are usually confronted about a quarter of the way into our lives.

We came into the workforce at a time when jobs were scarce, to put it lightly. I happily moved across the country when I was offered one and found myself in a city where I didn't know a soul. And did I mention it was really cold?

---

1   https://nypost.com/2017/11/15/majority-of-millennials-claim-to-be-in-a-quarter-life-crisis/

One of the biggest hurdles for me when I moved was making close friends. It took at least six months to feel like I had made any real connections, and I'm the kind of person who has no problem joining a soccer team, asking a new buddy to grab coffee, or a going to Bible study. I jump into those situations happily, but I know many people who shudder at the thought of it. For many people, making friends in a new city is a daunting task.

It was a lonely period at times, and I would talk to my mom quite often. Her words are still a nice reminder for me that some of my previously held beliefs about happiness weren't quite right.

"True happiness," she said, "will come from within. Be there for others. Stay focused. Be yourself. Do your best. And let God do the rest."

A big misconception I had about happiness, one that these words helped me work through, was that happiness and success were one in the same. We'll talk about that more in the next chapter, but for now, know this: This period of life looks different for everyone.

There are a million new and different experiences you could have. And if the sheer amount of quarter-life crises going on in this country are any indication, there's a good chance that you've been confronted with a situation that you thought would bring you happiness but that left you feeling disappointed.

Even though that sounds depressing, there's good news. Great news, even. Millennials *want* to be happy. However, we're open to a new definition of the word. We're open to trying new things to make ourselves the best we can be.

But there's something really big in our way . . .

THE COMPARISON GAME

Has this situation ever happened to you? You're scrolling through Facebook and you see an old friend, someone you've known for awhile but don't talk to regularly. Looks like she and her husband just bought a house and are expecting their second baby.

Wait a second, they just went on a trip to Bali two months ago. How can they afford a house like that?

And how are they both so in shape? If they're working high-enough paying jobs to afford that lifestyle, how do they still have time to go to the gym?

Ugh, and they have a Nespresso machine. Their lives are perfect. I can't look at this anymore.

Oh, look, an ex-boyfriend. And now he's engaged. Gooood. Great. I'm. So. Happy. For. Them.

Sound familiar? Maybe it's a tad dramatic. Or maybe this happened last night. Either way, the biggest hurdle to uncovering your own happiness is often comparing yourself to others. So don't do it. Problem solved. Let's move on.

Of course, I'm joking. If it were so easy to turn off our phones and ignore what everyone else was doing, we would have figured out how to break the habit by now. But the truth is that true happiness and fulfillment can only be achieved through a peace of mind that comes from deep in our souls. In other words, we need to reach a state of gratitude and acceptance that where we are in our lives is okay. We are *exactly* where we need to be.

And the way that we reach that is through continual self improvement. It's by creating new habits that will serve as daily reminders to focus on what matters. I'm not going to tell you to turn off your phone and ignore your successful friends. That would be rude, and quite frankly wrong. Remember, we're going to be talking about your network a lot in this book. Instead, I'm going to help you establish some methods for reminding yourself that you are exactly where you need to be and that you're on your way to where you want to go.

At the end of the day, comparing ourselves to others only leads to the same problem we're already facing. What happens when you, too, go to Bali? Or when you buy a house? Will you experience the same kind of joy that your friend did? Is it any different than your parents telling you that a steady job would be fulfilling?

We are a unique generation, the only one in existence to have grown up with the internet but to still have memories of a time before it. We remember using the home phone line to dial up the internet and have distinct memories of the AOL sound. You know the one I'm talking about.

To say that any of us knows what will make an entire generation happy, especially one like ours, is crazy. To figure that out, we can't look for a one-size-fits-all solution. We need to look inside and discover the answers for ourselves.

WHAT YOU CAN EXPECT

To put it simply, this book is going to help you do just that—look inside yourself and figure out what will make you fulfilled and happy—and then it's going to give you a roadmap to work toward that definition of happiness day by day. Because just like there's no one-size-fits-all solution, there's also no quick fix.

But I can promise you this: **If you truly commit, each day you will be better and happier than you were yesterday.**

I'll be honest here. This book won't replace professional help if you're experiencing depression. And it's not intended to help with intense grief. As I mentioned before, I haven't yet experienced that kind of pain and can't speak from experience about how to recover from it.

Instead, this book is about change. It's about building habits that will affect the everyday choices you make. It's about using the limited amount of time you have each day wisely. It's about finding joy and gratitude in the small things. Most of all, it's about getting to know yourself so that all the choices you make are intentional and add to your happiness, rather than bouncing from one thing to the next hoping to stumble on fulfillment.

MY MISSION STATEMENT

I'd like to share something with you now, a mission statement that I wrote for my life. I have it written down and tucked away in a few places—my desk, my nightstand. I try to keep it top of mind always. That way, when I'm faced with one of the hundreds of decisions we all have to make in a day, my mission statement can guide my choice. Here it is.

To live a faith-driven life focused on finding the good things in life and positively impacting those around me.

That last part is a big reason for writing this book. I believe deeply that this book will have a positive impact on those who read it and adopt its principles.

By the end of the book, it's my goal that you will have a clear idea of your life's mission. It sounds like a huge undertaking, but if I can do it, you can do it. I will help you understand your values, your goals, and your drive. Together, we'll uncover your long-term path to happiness. And in the last chapter, you'll write your own mission statement.

But before we move on, let me reiterate that it's okay to be exactly where you are right now. You don't need to know exactly who you are; you just need to be willing to invest in yourself and to understand that it's a lifelong journey.

Consider the Farmington River one last time. Sometimes, you're going to come across some rocks that will get in your way and slow you down. Other times, you'll come across some boulders that you'll need to find a path around. But no matter what, you will keep moving. Life, like a river, moves forward no matter what.

So if you don't think you're up for the effort of a lifelong journey, don't worry. Next, we're going to talk about how to make happiness a habit, one you won't need to think about as much as time goes by. But for now, all you need is the desire to change.

Let's get started.

CHAPTER 1

CHOOSING HAPPINESS

"Positive people don't just have a good day; they make it a good day."

—RICHARD BRANSON

WHEN MY WIFE, JOSLYN, AND I first started dating, I decided not to rush into telling her all about my goal to be better than I was yesterday. It was like you see on TV shows, when the best friend advises the main character not to come on too strong. Not to jump into his life's philosophy until months later, when he knows that they're compatible. I kept trying not to get ahead of myself.

I figured three dates was probably enough time.

I had already captured my thoughts in a short video that detailed my philosophy so that I could hear myself outloud, and I thought this would be perfect to show Joslyn. In it, I walked through each of the 5 Pillars that I'll talk about in this book, and I spent a lot of time talking about the idea that we can all choose to be happy. As you can imagine, sharing something so personal was a little scary. But I had a feeling about Joslyn, and I thought it would lead to a meaningful, special conversation.

We still laugh about it because we had just started dating, yet I had already presented her with cornerstones to my philosophy on life.

Looking back now, I'm sure she was thinking, *This handsome man has yet to experience real life! Happiness is a bit more complex than that.*

One important thing to know about Joslyn is that she has experienced deep loss, a pain I couldn't grasp fully when I met her. When she was sixteen, her father was diagnosed with cancer. A week after she moved into her dorm room as an eighteen-year-old college freshman, he passed away. And nearly a decade later, that loss and how it affected her family's dynamic still weighed heavily on her. It was something I was just coming to understand at this time in our relationship.

Shortly after I shared the video with her, we had a chance to go on a quick camping trip together. While sitting in front of the fire and toasting s'mores, many people would probably prefer to keep the conversation light. Not us—we decided to dive headlong into our outlooks on happiness.

I told her that I didn't necessarily understand why her dad's death still carried the same painful weight in her life. Hadn't time helped her heal? Hadn't she made choices that led her back to a happy place in her life since then?

Joslyn taught me that losing her father was a piece of her story. That it would always be a part of her life experience, pain included. She also told me that, eventually, I would likely go through a similar type of loss that would help me understand where someone with her experience was coming from and how someone with loss views happiness through a more complex lense.

You know, cheery bonfire conversation.

That night, she pushed me and tested all the beliefs I had held so tightly. I knew that she was right that I couldn't fully understand her perspective at that time, and she was also right that the pain she had already experienced would eventually find me, too. Hard times and loss are inevitable in this life.

As we continued dating, I learned more about Joslyn's dad. He was the kind of man everyone wanted to be around, the one people gravitated toward in a room. He would bring his family to church every weekend and was there for anyone in need. He was positive, kind, and upbeat. He was well-liked by many. Joslyn always tells me how much he would have enjoyed meeting me and I would have enjoyed getting to know him. I wish I had that opportunity.

Joslyn and her dad's favorite activity to do together was to go running. He had always hoped one of his kids would enjoy running as much as he did, and, lucky for him, Joslyn was that runner. She set school records at her high school, won state titles, and ran Division I cross country in college. They agreed to run a marathon together after Joslyn graduated.

That dream never came true for him. But Joslyn kept running.

It was her therapy, her way of working through the pain, of finding the space to ask God why this had happened to her family. When I came into the picture, running became a big part of our own relationship and eventually a major theme in our conversations about happiness.

On the tenth anniversary of her father's death, Jos and I signed up to run the New York City Marathon in his honor. We trained together just about every day and raised nearly ten thousand dollars for the Jimmy V Foundation for Cancer Research.

Still only months into our relationship, friends joked that I was crazy. It was a *huge* commitment to make, and even though I played Division I soccer in college, I was no distance runner. But when you know, you know. Joslyn was special, and I would have done anything for her. There was no way I wouldn't support her when it came to honoring her dad through the marathon.

The experience of training for the marathon changed both of us in some ways. I came to better understand her dedication to his memory and her drive to preserve it, even if it meant facing pain from time to time. And Jos began to see how, even in the face of pain, she could channel her feelings into something positive and take charge of her own happiness.

Truth be told, she says it best. Right before the marathon she wrote this in an essay for ESPN.com[2]:

In the midst of awesome friendships, incredible professional opportunities, and other bountiful blessings added to my young adult life, I had conditioned myself to view life's circumstances through a negative lens, verifying feelings by pointing back to my painful loss. As a result, I spent years feeding the fear that I would be unable to taste pure, positive, light-hearted joy through the calluses that cancer left on my soul.

I never viewed positivity as a choice. Instead, I believed one's mindset was something wholly sovereign. You either were a glass-half-full or glass-half-empty kind of person. It was out of one's control; a product of dealt cards. The thought of simple happiness made me curious, but I wasn't convinced it was for me.

I used to cling to the notion that it's the trials in life that make us stronger. After all, my loss did toughen me and help me ambitiously tackle the world in many ways. Recently, though, I've started to realize that perhaps it's not the trial after all—it's what we choose to do with the trial that strengthens us, grows us, and ultimately heals us.

Maybe, just maybe, it isn't my dad's cancer that created those calluses. It's our series of choices in response to trials that holds us down or lifts us up.

---

2   http://www.espn.com/espnw/athletes-life/article/11801438/
celebrate-my-father-memory-triumph-trials

No matter what we are faced with, we have the opportunity to choose happiness. When I first spoke to Jos about it, I implied that we could simply shake our bodies, change our mindsets, and be instantly happy. I understand, now more than ever, that that's not always the case. And I recognize that, while happiness is a choice, it's not always an easy one.

The ultimate goal of this book is to help you find a greater sense of fulfillment and happiness. I believe that the route to such happiness is through self improvement and, just as important, self awareness. But it begins with a choice.

You've already made the choice to pick up this book and have made it this far, so you're well on your way to choosing happiness. By the end of this chapter, I hope you'll be committed to that decision, so committed that you'll be ready to break the bad habits getting in your way and dig deep into understanding what will ultimately bring fulfillment.

But before we get there, let's spend some time talking about what happiness is (and what it isn't).

DEFINING HAPPINESS

When I started writing this chapter, I decided I would look for some quotes from famous thinkers about their definition of happiness. What I found was actually pretty comical. No one seems to agree about what it is or how we find it!

Here's a quick example. Aristotle said, "Happiness is the meaning and the purpose of life, the whole aim and end of human existence."

But Eleanor Roosevelt said, "Happiness is not a goal . . . it's a by-product of a life well lived."

And another. Anne Frank wrote, "Whoever is happy will make others happy."

But Martin Luther King Jr. said, "Those who are not looking for happiness are the most likely to find it, because those who are searching forget that the surest way to be happy is to seek happiness for others."

No wonder happiness is so hard for us to come by. Even some of the greatest minds in history disagree. As a society, we have no single definition of the word, and we certainly don't have a shared methodology for finding it.

All that said, I don't believe it's because happiness is so difficult to achieve that we can't agree on these things. Rather, it's because we're not all the same. Happiness looks different for each of us, and we will have different routes for achieving it. But for the sake of this book, let's clarify what I mean when I talk about happiness.

SUCCESS ≠ HAPPINESS

One thing that I quickly pick up on when people talk about happiness is that they're usually talking about success. When thinking about what will make them happy, they say things like a promotion, a bigger paycheck, a big house. The truth is that these are simply goals.

Now, I'm not knocking goals. They're super important to helping us achieve a happier, more fulfilled life. But they aren't the end product. It's like the trip to Bali. Once you've gone on it, what next? Have you found all the fulfillment you'll need in your life from that trip? Of course not. You're so much more than that.

The same goes for getting a promotion. You think if you can just push yourself harder, if you can just get your boss to appreciate your work, if you can get the paycheck you want, then you'll be happier. Sound familiar?

We all fall into that way of thinking from time to time. It's hard not to in the age of social media comparisons, but it's the *why* behind all of our goals that really drives happiness. To visualize this, let's take some common goals and successes and think about how they could really contribute to happiness.

SUCCESS	HAPPINESS
I want a promotion.	I'd like my job to give me a sense of fulfillment and impact.
I want more money.	I want to use the money I have on things that bring me—and others—happiness (charity, travel, family).
I want a nice car.	I enjoy the mechanics of cars and appreciate quality craftsmanship. I get a boost of happiness when I drive a well-built car.
I want a big house.	I love sharing my home with family and friends.
I want to travel.	I enjoy learning about and experiencing different cultures.

See how easy it is for success and happiness to become intertwined? Chances are that we all want to achieve one or two of these goals or something similar. If your work brings you happiness, why wouldn't you want to dive deeper into it through a promotion? And if you love hosting your family for Christmas, a big house may be a priority for you. Goals are *good*.

It's when we blindly try to achieve all of these goals without understanding why we want them that they come up feeling hollow. If we're looking for our car to be a status symbol or are mostly looking forward to a trip because of the photos we'll be able to post, we're not likely to find happiness in them.

And, at the risk of sounding like a broken record, let me repeat: **Happiness looks different for everyone.**

I chose the goals above because I hear them so often. They harken back to those definitions of happiness we've had handed down to us, don't they? The house. The family. The steady job. Mom and Dad may be proud if you reach them. But will you be happy? Will you be fulfilled?

So if happiness and successes aren't the same, then how do we define happiness?

THE FRUIT OF THE SPIRIT

My faith plays a huge role in my personal happiness. Research does suggest that being a part of a religious community can add to your overall happiness, and we will talk about spirituality in more depth later on.[3] Even if you don't share my Christian beliefs, you may find some value in what I have learned through my experience.

There is a verse in the book of Galatians in the Bible that reads, "But the fruit of the Spirit is love, joy, peace, patience, kindness, goodness, faithfulness, gentleness, self-control; against such things there is no law."

When I think about happiness, the Fruit of the Spirit is the first thing that comes into my mind. Love, joy, peace . . . Those are the building blocks of overall happiness and fulfillment. They are welcomed outcomes to achieving our goals. They can ground the reasons behind why we make the choices we do.

Will this bring me joy? Will I be at peace with myself if I do that? Will others be kind to me if I treat them this way? Will I experience all the gentleness and goodness that the people around me have to offer? These

---

3   https://money.usnews.com/money/personal-finance/articles/2012/04/12/
    religion-makes-people-happierbut-why

are some basic questions we can ask ourselves as we guide our attitudes and actions.

Whether you're a practicing Christian or not, it's useful to consider the Fruit of the Spirit when talking about happiness. The definition of Fruit in this case simply means the product of something, the result or effect. In this specific context, it means the result of being aligned with the Holy Spirit. It sticks out to me because it reminds me that every action we take has an effect. How we choose to act may bring us joy, or it may cause jealousy. Our choices may bring goodness, or they may bring anger. But ultimately they are our choices to make.

The path to happiness and fulfillment will be filled with countless decisions, both big and small. As we go down it, we have to think about every choice in terms of cause and effect. We have to study the decisions that resulted in joy or goodness or peace. And we have to understand the ones that brought us insecurity or disappointment.

It takes practice at first, along with a lot of experimentation, patience, and persistence. But at the end of the day, your alignment will lead you to true happiness and real fulfillment. And now, without any further ado, here's my definition of happiness. Ready?

True happiness is peace of mind deep in your soul that stems from your actions aligning with your values, dreams and relationships, ultimately resulting in love, joy, peace, patience, kindness, goodness, faithfulness, gentleness, and self-control for yourself and others.

Even within that definition, the idea of choice is implied. Happiness can be found through our own actions, through how we align ourselves. It's about controlling what we are able to and finding peace in the decisions we can make. And it's about being honest with ourselves.

And fulfillment, you ask? How is that different?

Fulfillment is happiness held for a prolonged period of time. You can find happiness in small, isolated moments. But fulfillment is about understanding your values and *consistently* acting in accordance with them. Fulfillment, my friends, is our ultimate goal.

If you feel like you're already there, great! And if you think you've got a ways to go, that's fantastic. No matter where you are in your own journey, we can get there together. And good news: It isn't just a hunch of mine. There are scientific studies that support the idea that we have control over our happiness.

THE SCIENCE OF CHOICE

Actions and results. Cause and effect. So that's the basis for overall happiness and fulfillment. But does it mean that we have complete control over 100% of our happiness? Do I deny that other factors can affect happiness, too? Absolutely not. Joslyn's story is a perfect example of that. Her father's death had a deep impact on her happiness, and it was completely out of her hands.

When I think about choosing happiness, I like to think of the quote by Charles R. Swindoll, which says, "I am convinced that life is 10% what happens to me and 90% of how I react to it."

Is that number steeped in science? Nope, but it speaks to the idea that happiness can't be explained away by any one factor. Things like genetics and life events can have an effect on happiness, yes, but so can our choices.

According to two recent studies, researchers found that participants who were told to try to feel happier could actually elevate their moods. Just by *trying* to do so.[4]

Likewise, a study found that workers who smiled as a result of cultivating positive thoughts improved their moods and experienced less withdrawal from work than those who were fake smiling.[5]

---

4   https://www.alphagalileo.org/ViewItem.aspx?ItemId=134259&CultureCode=en
5   https://www.eurekalert.org/pub_releases/2011-02/msu-sfa022211.php

And in *The How of Happiness*, author Sonja Lyubomirsky applies her studies of twins and their happiness to show that, while genes and circumstance play a real role in happiness, we also have a profound amount of control over our happiness through our choices.

But again, we can't snap our fingers and find happiness and fulfillment. Choosing a happier life doesn't typically happen in an instant. We have to make choices every day that we know will affect our happiness, and we have to remain aware of how that happiness will shift over time.

There's a line I love in a recent *TIME* article about happiness. The author writes, "We have designated work hours. We schedule doctor appointments. Heck, we even schedule hair appointments.

"We say happiness is the most important thing but fail to consistently include it in our calendars."[6]

I love the image of penciling in happiness on our calendars, giving it equal billing to things like paying bills and eating lunch. Truth be told, if you're looking for real change, some planning and scheduling will be necessary, at least at first.

Choosing happiness needs to become second nature, a habit, and habits aren't easy to change. It's why the diet and fitness industries are such giants. Adopting new eating habits takes work, and when one diet fails, there's another promising a quick fix. They try to get around the idea that quick fixes rarely result in permanent change when, in fact, it takes an average of 28 days to change a habit. And as you keep reading, remember this: Motivation is what gets you started. Habit is what keeps you going.

But don't worry. In the next chapter, we'll go through habit forming in more detail, and you'll have a game plan in place as you head into the chapters on the 5 Pillars. For now, know this: The payoff of changing your habits will be huge. You will finally be prioritizing your happiness

---

6   http://time.com/2933943/the-8-things-the-happiest-people-do-every-day/

the way you do hair appointments and doctor visits. You will take owner-ship over the areas of your life that you can control. And it will get easier over time.

Take it from someone who has run a marathon—training yourself to be happier won't be nearly as painful as the first month of running was for me. Maybe you've quit smoking or stopped biting your nails or started reading one book per month. Whatever it is, you've changed a habit before, and you can do it again. And remember, the end goal is joy and peace and kindness. So by all means, please, I beg of you, have some fun with it!

Now, let's talk about these 5 Pillars. What the heck are they?

THE 5 PILLARS

Picture the Parthenon, if you will. And if you've forgotten what that looks like, go ahead and Google it. Do you notice all the stone pillars? When we talk about each Pillar, I'd like you to visualize them.

The 5 Pillars that we'll talk about in this book are as follows:

- ‣ Physical
- ‣ Mental
- ‣ Emotional
- ‣ Spiritual
- ‣ Professional

Together, these Pillars make up different foundational areas of our lives where joy and goodness and the remaining fruits of fulfillment can be found. I narrowed it down to these areas by paying attention to studies and research about happiness, talking with the people around me, and, yes, through a healthy dose of personal experience. And I've found that if any one falls apart or crumbles, it's likely to have a domino effect on the others.

So you see, it's like a house. Or an ancient temple. The Parthenon was built in 447 B.C. and is still (mostly) standing today thanks to the pillars that have provided strength and stability to it for centuries.

But when it comes to fulfillment, each Pillar doesn't need to carry equal weight. Some people may value mental growth over physical growth, and that's great. They could place a bigger emphasis on improving mentally if they wanted.

But if they ignored their physical life completely, cutting down on sleep and avoiding the gym or exercising, it would start to catch up with them. They'd lose energy and their overall happiness would take a hit.

All 5 Pillars play a role in our day-to-day happiness and long-term fulfillment, but it's up to us to figure out their importance in our own lives. To do that, we'll go through them one at a time.

I've ordered them in a way so that they'll build on one another. We'll start out with the Physical Pillar because it's vital to our health and happiness. It's also one that may have some visual effects to show for your efforts.

Then we'll move into the Mental Pillar and focus on expanding our knowledge bases and curiosity.

The Emotional Pillar will deal with responding to circumstances around us and processing the emotions that naturally come up in response.

From there, we'll move up to the Spiritual Pillar. If you think about the 5 Pillars in terms of Maslow's hierarchy of needs, you can see how we're moving along from baseline needs to higher-level, more existential thought.

And we'll end by talking about the Professional Pillar. Maslow may not classify it as his highest level (after all, we do need a paycheck to survive in the modern era), but it is the area where we'll inevitably spend most of our time. And since we're spending upwards of 8 hours a day focusing on this area, it's also where we may have the biggest opportunity to make an impact.

In the next chapter, we'll talk about how to change your habits using these 5 Pillars. The first month after picking up this book will be spent in a period of exploration and habit forming. I'll give you some daily challenges in each Pillar that you can choose from to push yourself out of your comfort zone and to find out what drives your individual happiness. From day one, you will start down the journey of being better than you were the day before.

But before we do that, I'd like to leave you with a hypothetical scenario to consider. I mentioned in the introduction that moving to Hartford, CT, was a shock to my system. The climate, the people, the culture. It was all different from what I was used to growing up and in college, but I chose to make the best of it. I tried my hardest to find happiness and joy in a setting that was, at times, off-putting to my southern sensibilities. But moving to a new city is nothing unique to me. So many of us do it all the time, whether by choice or because work opportunities demand it. Let's think through how my mindset could have changed my experience.

SCENARIO ONE

You move into your new apartment in Hartford. You're overwhelmed and tired, so you avoid eye contact in the hallways as you bring boxes into your new place. You spend all your free time unpacking boxes and taking trips to the store for things you need. It's not until your first day of work that you actually talk to someone.

On your way home, drivers cut you off left and right. At the grocery store, no one looks up from their phones or their shopping lists. God forbid someone hold a door open for someone else.

You go to work happy hours and struggle to join in the conversation. You feel like an outsider, and the next time they ask, you pretend that you have plans to avoid sitting there awkwardly.

A few months go by, you've finished watching every episode of *The Office* for the third time, and you find yourself wondering how it is that everyone around you has friends. Where do they meet these people? Are they just better conversationalists than you? Maybe it's just the culture. They're not as friendly here.

When your parents call to check on you, you lie and say that you're doing fine. You actually need to hang up because you have dinner plans to get ready for. In reality, it's another frozen pizza that's waiting.

More time goes by. Nothing changes. You start to look for jobs closer to home.

SCENARIO TWO

You spend your first week in a new city saying hello to everyone who makes eye contact with you. And those that don't. You meet a few people in the building who have dogs, like you do, and meet up again at the neighborhood dog park.

When you go to work happy hours, you jump in when you have something to say but try to be patient. Eventually, all the inside jokes will be replaced with new ones, hopefully ones that you'll will be a part of.

After a month, you sign up for a soccer league. You played in high school, so hopefully it will be a nice way to meet people. You try out a few different churches in the area, looking for one that seems right for you. And when you find it, you join a small group.

You make a promise to yourself that you won't turn on the television for a week. Doing so forces you to read the book your coworker recommended or call the neighbor you met at the dog park.

Slowly, deeper friendships form. You realize that, even though the culture is different than what you're used to, the people are still good and interesting and engaging. You start to feel comfortable, happy even.

Choices are all around us. All day, every day we make them. And for the most part, we make them without thinking. We live in a state of auto-pilot. If I had followed scenario 1 myself, who's to say where I'd be right now? But I can tell you one thing—I wouldn't be married to Joslyn. Without keeping myself open to new opportunities and happiness, I wouldn't have found the person who makes me happiest of all.

Let's get out of that pattern of autopilot decisions. Let's start putting consciousness behind our choices. Let's be intentional about how we act. Let's break the habits that hold us back.

Here's how we'll do it.

CHAPTER 2

CHANGING HABITS

"Happiness is a choice that requires effort at times."

—AESCHYLUS

TO DEMONSTRATE THE SHEER amount of choices that we make without thinking in a given day, I've got a series of questions for you.

As you go through these, don't think about why you do these things, just take note of *what* you do and try to be as specific as possible. When asked about the first thing you do each morning, you may be tempted to say that you go for a run. But before that, you may actually check your phone, wash your face, or lace up your shoes in a particular chair. Get granular with your answers, and don't be afraid to mark up these pages if you want.

Ready?

1 What is the *very* first thing you do each morning?

2 When you get ready in the morning, do you brush your teeth or wash your face first?

3 When you style your hair or shave your facial hair, do you start on one side of your face?

4 If you make coffee, what's your first step (i.e., grabbing a filter or going to the sink for water)?

5 When you drive to work, what route do you take?

6 When you get to work, what do you do first?

Now, let's pause for a second. Don't just breeze past these questions—take a few moments to answer them honestly. One of the very first steps in changing habits is acknowledging them, and if you're looking for a happier lifestyle, this exercise is your very first challenge in achieving it. Embrace it!

In the course of only a couple hours after waking up, you can see just how many small, seemingly insignificant choices we are all faced with. Do you spend a few minutes checking Facebook when you first wake up, or are you out of bed the second your alarm clock goes off? Do you watch *Good Morning America* while you sip your coffee, do you have a podcast going as you get ready, or do you prefer some quiet in the morning? Do you go for a morning jog, or do you scramble out the door fifteen minutes after getting up?

And how many times have you tried to change up that routine and failed?

I myself used to be a chronic snoozer. It took three or four alarms, going off every five minutes, to get me up in the morning. And with a wakeup time of 4:30 a.m., you can imagine how hard that was on Joslyn. She was usually my final alarm, nudging me to roll out of bed instead of staying in it through multiple snooze cycles.

One day, I bought one of those analog alarm clocks. I placed it just out of reach, so that I'd have to get up to shut it off, and I gave it a nickname. I decided that rather than call it an alarm clock, I'd refer to it as my "opportunity clock." It was my reminder to get my day started and do the things I had planned for that morning. Once I was out of bed, I would have the opportunity to go on a run or take my dog on a long walk or make the coffee.

At first, I kept it up because it made me chuckle. I'd make jokes about my opportunity clock to Joslyn and tell her what I planned to do when it went off. At first, when it would start to ring in the morning (in that particularly harsh outdated alarm clock way), I'd grumble and then remember its funny name and laugh to myself. And then, almost magically, I'd remember those things I wanted to do that morning. Suddenly those activities seemed more fun than going back to bed for ten more minutes. And over time, something great happened.

I stopped thinking about it.

When the opportunity clock went off, I'd get up, turn it off, and head to the bathroom to brush my teeth. I didn't laugh at it as much, but I also didn't snooze it. Despite waking up relatively early for years, it was the first time that I felt like I could really, honestly call myself a morning person.

That's the beautiful and difficult thing about habits. On one hand, they save us a lot of time and effort. How tedious would our mornings be if we had to think about how to put toothpaste on our toothbrushes or really think through the steps of making coffee? Being in a state of autopilot allows us to enjoy the music on the radio during our commutes instead of thinking about where to turn next. It allows us the space to think about the day ahead.

On the other hand, habits are difficult to change. While the desire to change a habit can happen in the blink of an eye, it takes awareness and a lot of repetition to make an action second nature. I know that I couldn't quit snoozing my alarms until I started paying attention to that goal, practicing that action, and enjoying the rewards that came from waking up earlier.

Where habits and happiness start to come into conflict is when we think that the actions we're taking are decisions when they are, in fact, habits. One study found that as much as 40% of our actions in a given day were due to habits, not conscious decision-making.

Think back to your morning ritual. Performing those actions without much thought saves you time, but if you wanted to, you could throw that plan in the trash tomorrow morning and do something entirely different. Instead of rushing out the door, you could go watch the sunrise. You could part your hair to a different side. You could go paddleboarding. You could roll around the house on Rollerblades while getting ready. You have endless choices!

Now think about how many more choices you have over the course of an entire day. None of your behavior patterns are set in stone. You could change them at any time, so long as you're able to form new habits to replace them. And those new habits, if carefully thought through, could bring you huge amounts of joy.

That's what it's all about—thinking big about your values and what you want in life and doing things day after day to support them. Over time, after those new actions become habit, finding happiness won't feel so hard. But it's only by bringing awareness to your habits that you can start to change them. So how exactly do we do it?

Glad you asked.

HOW TO FORM A HABIT

In Charles Duhigg's book *The Power of Habit*, he explains that there are three components to all habits: a cue, an action, and a reward.

The cue is your trigger to start your habit. If you're a foot tapper, your cue may be feeling nervous. You may have a test coming up that is causing you stress. So while you study, your toe taps against the desk leg without thinking. Or when you're out of school, maybe you're about to ask your boss for a raise and you're nervous about the response. Suddenly the toe tap comes back.

In this example, the toe tap is the action. But what, then, is the reward? Maybe it's a sense of calm that comes from the rhythmic sensation of it or just having a channel for your nervous energy. Rewards come in all shapes and sizes, and they can be surprising. If you're a snoozer like I was, the reward may be that feeling when your eyes start to close again and you give in to sleep.

In his book, Duhigg also explains that products like shampoo foam and lather solely to create a reward sensation. We *feel* like we have cleaner hair as a result of it, but the foam serves no purpose. So as you start to form new habits, don't be fooled into thinking that rewards can only mean treating yourself to a new purchase or eating sweets. They can be just about anything that makes you feel good or accomplished.

When you're looking to form a new habit, make sure that you keep all three components in mind, especially the reward. Over time, you'll start to crave that reward, which will help keep the habit going.

Let's look at an example together.

Let's say that you've decided you want to read more. It's a noble goal, and one that I fully support since I want you to make it to the end of this book. Think about the last time you really enjoyed reading, when you had fun with it or thought to yourself, *I should do this more often.*

What was it that you enjoyed so much? Was it a particular genre that you don't often read? Or was it the setting? Maybe you were in a hammock with a drink in hand or in a quiet nook in your house, curled up with a blanket. Maybe it was just a feeling of escape from thinking about your to-do list. Think about what made the experience enjoyable and consider if you can replicate that feeling in some way.

If you're the vacation hammock reader, it may not be possible to recreate your circumstances every day. But think about what else you do that relaxes you. Maybe that means being in nature, so you could find a park bench or head to your backyard when the weather's nice. Maybe it's the quiet of the vacation that you liked, in which case turn off the TV and music and try reading in silence.

It's about capturing the *feeling* you experienced when you enjoyed reading. That's your reward, and there are endless options at your disposal for how to conjure those feelings again.

The other part of the habit-changing equation is time. Repetition is key to changing habits, and it takes about 28 days to train your brain into adopting a new pattern of behavior and for a habit to really take hold. So while you may need to get yourself into the habit of reading every evening by clearing off your nightstand of everything but a book, eventually the action of getting into bed will cue the habit of reading.

This process of breaking bad habits and forming new ones is how you'll be able to grow day after day. To continue to be better than you were yesterday. When performing actions that bring you joy start to become second nature, you open up headspace to push further, to form new habits in a different area of your life, to continue growing and building toward fulfillment.

WHERE DO WE GO FROM HERE?

If all of that sounds a little overwhelming, don't worry. I'm not just going to send you off to change all your habits right now. We're going to spend some time together, exploring what exactly is going to make *you* happy (remember, it's different for everyone) and practicing bringing awareness to our existing habits.

And we're going to do this through some daily challenges.

At the end of each chapter describing a different Pillar, there will be a month's worth of challenges for you. They may include things like:

▸ Say hi to a stranger today.

▸ Take stairs wherever possible today.

▸ Read a selection of a religious text from your faith. Or, if you don't practice, try reading a selection from one that interests you.

▸ Ask someone you admire professionally to have coffee.

▸ Cook a meal from a culture or cuisine you don't normally eat.

▸ Give two compliments today, one to someone you know and the other to someone you don't.

▸ Park in a different location at the office, grocery store, or gym.

▸ Try out a new podcast.

The goal of these challenges is to help you kickstart change and to get you thinking about your happiness every day. **I recommend that you start each morning by picking one challenge from the chapter you're currently reading.** By doing so, the very first new habit you'll form will be starting each morning with an opportunity to choose happiness.

If it's difficult to remember, create a note for yourself and put it somewhere you know you'll see first thing, like on top of your phone or posted to the wall nearby. Write down, "Today, I will be better than I was the day before." Let that be your cue to pick up the book and get to it.

As you go, be sure to pay attention to how you're feeling. Circle or highlight any activities that brought you particular joy. Later on, you may want to recapture that feeling. So please, have some fun with it and choose things that are a little outside of your comfort zone. Above all, make this book your own. Because change never truly occurs inside ones comfort zone; step outside of it.

Experimentation is really the name of the game during this period. You're figuring out what brings you happiness, and you're identifying which of the 5 Pillars are most important to you. I'm a firm believer that if you ignore one Pillar entirely, it will have a negative domino effect on the others. But it is okay to dabble in some, while really embracing others.

The ultimate goal is that, by the time you have finished reading this book, you'll have a clear understanding of your personal values and will have set some goals for yourself. You'll then create a month-long schedule of personal daily challenges, based around those values. And one morning, as if by magic, you'll wake up with an awareness that you hold the keys to your own happiness in your hands.

WHAT IF I STUMBLE?

I've said before that this won't all happen overnight. For most of us, change takes time and effort, and there are likely going to be some roadblocks along the way. You might oversleep one morning and forget to pick a challenge, or you may have a rough day at work that stops you from completing the one you've picked out. It's totally normal to have some setbacks. Unfortunately, it's also totally normal for us to freak out about it, call ourselves failures, and throw in the towel.

When we kick ourselves for not going on that morning run or for giving into the temptation of a third cup of coffee, we tend to think of our failures as weaknesses. *I didn't run because I'm lazy.* Or, *I wasn't able to cut back on caffeine because I have to have it to get through the day.* And once we start getting down on ourselves, it's a downward spiral from there.

Negative thoughts are a huge impediment to changing habits. And they're also what we're trying to avoid! We're on a quest for happiness and fulfillment. Negative thoughts are just going to get in your way.

So as you start to push yourself to do new things, to think in new ways, remember that you're going to be coming up against all of your old habits. And don't worry, there are several ways to get yourself back on track.

The first thing to do is to give yourself some grace. Remember that where you are right now is enough. Where you would have been tomorrow is one step closer to your overall goal, not necessarily at the finish line. Take a few moments to think about what you are grateful for. Even on the worst days, you can find something in your life worth celebrating, and doing this will help get your mindset back to a positive place where you'll be more likely to pick back up.

And do you remember that note you posted by your bedside? The one telling you to be better than you were yesterday? Don't underestimate the power of visual reminders to get you back on track. Try putting it in a more prominent spot to make sure you pick your challenge in the morning.

Make a few other notes to help remind you of your challenge or goals throughout the day. Place them somewhere you know you'll see in your office, in your car, or even in your cell phone. Think about where you are when you tend to lose steam. Do you get frustrated at work and decide to cancel plans with friends or skip your spin class after work? Pay attention to what triggers those kinds of responses and head them off with a positive reminder.

Inspirational quotes are my personal favorite, and there are no shortage of them floating around the internet (or at the beginning of each chapter in this book). Find a few that resonate with you, and keep them front and center. Before you roll your eyes at it, try it out for a few days. I think you'll be surprised by the power that some well-placed reminders can have.

My last piece of advice if you get off track is to remember that change won't happen in a vacuum. The people you surround yourself with can have an enormous impact on your goals, both positive and negative. I'm a firm believer that "Your network is your net worth." The friends, family, and colleagues around us every day play into who we are and what we accomplish.

So try to surround yourself with the people whom you admire, whether for their smarts or positivity or spiritual connection. You don't have to cut anyone from your life that don't fall into that category, but explore forming deeper connections with the people who do. Because when you get stuck or you feel down on yourself, those will be the people that will likely be able to offer some helpful advice or support to get you out of that mindset. And you're going to hear me talk about mentors and support systems in each of the 5 Pillars, so start thinking about your network now.

Community is key. But whether you have a built-in support system with your friends and family or not, I'm here to offer you another.

THE ALWAYSSMILIN COMMUNITY

AlwaysSmilin is a lifestyle brand that I started, and it's mission is simple. We're there to spread positive vibes into the world. With everything going on these days, it's difficult to turn on the TV or read the news without ending up in a negative mood. So we want to be a beacon of light in all that negativity and help people embrace the incredible power of their own choices.

We've spent so much of this book talking about all the ways we have control over our own happiness, but sometimes you just need a helpful reminder of that fact. That's what AlwaysSmilin is there to do. We've built a community around the idea of positivity, and we'd like you to be a part of it. Here's how to get involved.

ALWAYSSMILIN.COM

Our website is the hub of all AlwaysSmilin activity. There you'll find any additional resources mentioned in this book, along with blog posts and videos to keep you motivated. You can also sign up for our newsletter, which will deliver positive messages to your inbox every week, or pick up some AlwaysSmilin swag.

SOCIAL MEDIA

Every day, we're posting challenges and quotes to inspire you. We're also sharing helpful articles about happiness and wellness. The goal is to be a positive reminder that we're in this together, that your happiness is in your control, and that you've got this. So follow us at @AlwaysSmilinHQ on Instagram and Twitter and get your daily dose of happy.

But this isn't just a one-sided affair. We want to hear from you, too! Are you making progress on your journey to be better than you were the day before? Tag us in your pictures, use the hashtag #alwayssmilinprogress, send us a good old-fashioned letter. Whatever it takes. We want to know what you're up to and send some good vibes and support your way.

And last but not least, use our social channels to get to know each other. Share a positive quote with a friend who could use it. Leave comments and encouragement for people using the hashtag.

AlwaysSmilin is there for you in whatever way you need it, whether that's just a small morale boost or as a full-blown community of supporters. **You're not alone on this journey.**

Keep that in mind as we head into the Physical Pillar and as you start taking on daily challenges. It may be tempting to skip a day when things get busy, and when that happens, draw some inspiration from the AlwaysSmilin community. Lean on them on tough days, and give it back to the community on days when you're feeling great.

And remember: You've got this. You have everything you need inside of you to be happy. You are a champ.

Now, let's have some fun.

CHAPTER 3

THE PHYSICAL PILLAR

"Take care of your body. It's the only place you have to live."

−JIM ROHN

THIS WAS A BAD IDEA. Maybe I should leave. Why did I think this would be a good idea? Why do I get myself into situations like this? I should leave. No, I should pick a spot in the back where no one can see me. Oh no, it's starting.

How did I end up in this situation? And what was I doing? Before we get there, let's take a little trip down memory lane.

I started playing soccer when I was just four years old. I remember my parents shuttling my siblings and me around to practices and games on the weekends. At that age, we all chased the ball in a clump, running as fast as we could because running was just plain fun.

I kept playing all the way through college for the Division I varsity team at Appalachian State University. Soccer was still fun, but long gone were the days of blindly chasing the ball around the field. Conditioning our bodies to be in peak physical shape was the goal. As was, of course, winning games. To prepare, we'd lift weights, swim laps, run up hills so steep we had to use our hands. And there was running. So much running.

If you've ever watched a soccer game, you know that running is key to the sport. And in my position as center back, I needed to be fast and have stamina. So I worked hard at it and took conditioning seriously. I wanted to be able to run faster than anyone I came up against in a game.

After graduation, things changed quickly. I no longer had a coach telling me exactly which exercises to do each day and pushing me to my limits. On top of that, I no longer had anyone to compete against at a high level. There were no matches coming up, no tournaments to prepare for. For the first time in my life, my fitness was just for the sake of fitness.

At first, this newfound freedom was liberating. I got into a routine of heading to the gym in the mornings before work, lifting some weights, and running. It was freeing to do the exercises I liked doing when I wanted to do them.

It didn't take long for that feeling of freedom to turn into boredom. I was doing the same exercises day in and day out. On top of that, I didn't feel like my health or fitness was progressing. I had hit a plateau.

In the interest of being better than I was the day before, I knew that I couldn't just keep on with more of the same. I needed a new challenge. I needed to find a way to push myself beyond my comfort zone. And I needed to find the inspiration to do that without the motivation of a coach. So I decided to experiment with my workouts. Instead of hitting the weights one morning, I'd go swimming. Rather than go on another treadmill run, I'd challenge myself to go on a particularly hilly hike.

I also started something new: hot yoga. That's right. I went in big with my very first yoga class, starting out with a 90-minute class in a room that was heated to 105 degrees. And man, was that a frightening experience at first. I had no idea what any of the words the instructor said meant. I didn't understand the breathing exercises or any of the poses the instructor called out. The room was so hot it was hard to take a deep breath. Not to mention, there were only a few other guys in there, and I was the only one not wearing a Speedo-inspired outfit.

This was a bad idea, I thought.

I didn't think I belonged. And after the first few seconds in the room, it was tempting to bail on the class entirely. I could pretend I was sick and that the heat was too much. I could make it to my regular gym and get a few miles in on the treadmill. But that was more of the same, and more of the same was *exactly* what I was trying to avoid. So I stuck it out.

I'll pick a spot in the back where no one can see me.

Throughout that class, I had no idea what I was doing. When we practiced balancing on one foot, I stumbled a few times and was convinced I'd eventually crash land into the woman next to me. The heat was intense, and I was sweating like I was back at soccer practice in the heat of a Texas or North Carolina summer. When we stretched, I was miles away from touching my toes.

Why do I get myself into situations like this?

But you know what? Every time I wobbled or accidentally inhaled my own sweat, I didn't get frustrated. I laughed to myself. This was *fun*. It was exciting to try something new, and it was even better that it was hard for me. It gave me something to work at, and so I added it into my new routine, trying to make it to class at least two or three times a week.

As time went by, I like to think that I got pretty good at yoga. My yoga vocabulary slowly increased, and my fingers inched closer to my toes. I also lost the weight that I'd set a goal to drop. Looking back, I can see that my body needed to have a shock to its system in order to see progress and to move past that plateau. I could have continued pushing myself in my old routine, running farther or lifting heavier weights. But I can see now how the variety in my fitness routine made me healthier in ways I hadn't considered. For instance, my body felt better after yoga's deep stretches, and I worked muscles I had forgotten about.

So why do I tell you all of this?

Well, in this chapter we're going to talk about some of the benefits to being physically fit, or at least healthier than you were the day before. This doesn't necessarily mean that each day you should run a few steps farther than you did the day before, the end goal being that you can run across the country like Forrest Gump. It's about finding a healthy balance by introducing variety into your life. It's about setting goals for yourself (and meeting them). And it's about making health something you think about every single day.

Now, it would take an incredibly dedicated person to pay equal attention to all aspects of their health, like exercise, diet, and sleep, and to maintain their peak performance all at once. We're human, and our focus shifts around depending on our current goals and life circumstances. When sleep gets out of whack, we may focus on getting more of it, even if it means sacrificing a few workouts. And after a vacation full of relaxation and delicious food, we may set stricter guidelines for healthy eating for ourselves.

In an ideal world, your physical health would look like someone spinning three plates—representing physical activity, healthy eating, and sleep—on individual poles. They'd spin at the same speed and never topple. This would be a perfect healthy equilibrium. But as mere mortals, what often happens is that when one plate starts to wobble, we pay greater attention to straightening it out until another one wobbles, demanding our attention again. We shift between them constantly.

The goal of this chapter is to help you do two things. The first is to question your current definition of health, to get you to try new things and explore other areas of health and fitness. And the second is to get you in the habit of thinking about all three areas of health more regularly, so that you don't have to wait for a plate to wobble or break before giving it your attention. You can preemptively head off those issues through greater awareness of your health.

I'm not a doctor, a nutritionist, or a personal trainer, so I'm not planning to present you with a diet or training plan. Rather, the goal of the Physical Pillar is to inspire you to seek greater health because your health has a profound impact on all of the other aspects of life. As I like to tell people, your health is your wealth. Give it the time and effort it deserves.

WHY IS THIS THE FIRST PILLAR?

We're starting off with the Physical Pillar for exactly the reason I just mentioned: its impact on all other areas of your life. When we're healthier, we're happier and more productive. We have better focus. We feel more energized.

And when all three areas of health are in harmony? Well, then there's nothing we can't do. The next four Pillars will be focused more on mental and emotional work. We're going to need to be at the top of our game, feeling focused and positive, to be able to tackle them together.

So let's start with the easiest area of health to improve: physical activity. I know what you're thinking. *Aaron, there's no way this is easier than getting more sleep.* To that I say, you're overthinking what physical activity is! It's not reserved for the bodybuilder types in the gym. Physical activity can be as simple as taking the stairs instead of the elevator or walking the dog. Let's look at why it's so important.

PHYSICAL ACTIVITY

Have you ever dreaded the idea of going to a workout class only to leave it feeling great? That's the power physical activity can have. When endorphins are released during exercise, they trigger positive feelings akin to euphoria. Ever heard of a "runner's high?" Well you don't have to run tons of miles to get a boost in mood. Even a long walk can improve your mood for most of the day.

Studies also show that there's a link between physical activity and mental sharpness. When we exercise, we see all kinds of mental benefits from increased concentration to better memory. We learn faster and have more mental stamina.[7]

There are so many benefits to physical activity, and we haven't even touched on physical health yet. In addition to improving our moods and mental acuity, physical activities can help prevent some of the country's leading causes of death, like heart disease and stroke.

Let's stop to consider that fact a little more. According to the Center for Disease Control, nearly 610,000 people in the U.S. die from heart disease every year. That's one in every four deaths. It may feel like heart disease is something to worry about way down the road, when we're older and nearing retirement. So why think about it now?

First of all, we already know that changing habits can be difficult. So it's better to start forming healthy habits earlier than later, when you may be at serious risk. More than that, this is *your* life, and all of the choices you make now will impact your health down the road. We have no control over how some things in life will go, whether disease or other struggles will come our way. But we have to give ourselves the best chance of a long and happy life, and we have to do what it takes to enjoy that life to its fullest along the way. That starts now.

So how much physical activity is enough then? Should we all strive to be ultramarathon runners or bodybuilders? Thankfully, the American Heart Association has some pretty simple guidelines. First, they define physical activity as "*anything* that makes you move your body and burn calories." So it doesn't have to be 100% cardio, like walking or biking. That description also includes activities like strength training and stretching.

---

7   https://hbr.org/2014/10/regular-exercise-is-part-of-your-job

And they recommend 150 minutes of activity per week. Put simply, that's 30 minutes, five times a week. Totally doable, right?

The American Heart Association also suggests that the easiest way to get started with physical activity is through walking. No expensive gym membership is required, and your day is full of opportunities to walk more. I always laugh when I go to the gym and see people circling the parking lot, looking for the closest spot to the entrance. I always want to tell them, "You're there to workout—walk a little farther!"

So when you go to the grocery store or to work or the gym, don't be that person. Walk a little more. Incorporate more movement into your everyday life. Try something new. Here are a few other ideas to get you started.

TIPS TO GET MOVING

- ▸ **PUT IT ON YOUR CALENDAR.** You're much more likely to do something if you block off time for it. Instead of trying to squeeze in a workout when everything else is done, schedule it and stick to your schedule.

- ▸ **START WITH EXERCISES YOU ENJOY DOING.** If you dread working out, you're going to lose momentum fast. Do you like being outside? Go for a hike. Go kayaking. Working out doesn't have to mean only running on a treadmill at the gym.

- ▸ **GO TO A FITNESS CLASS AND TRY SOMETHING NEW.** Not sure what you like? Try out some fitness classes and find something that works for you. Services like Classpass can be great for exploring your interests.

- ▸ **SET REWARDS. DO SOMETHING SATISFYING AFTER EACH WORKOUT.** Don't forget that rewards are critical to establishing habits. Treat yourself to a smoothie, listen to your favorite song, watch the sun rise or set, or even just take a few moments to enjoy the endorphins pumping through your body.

▸ **DON'T FORGET TO STRETCH AND TAKE REST DAYS.** Stretching and rest are so important. Don't push yourself too hard too fast, or you'll risk burnout and fatigue.

▸ **GRAB A FRIEND.** Do you do better with an accountability buddy? Or just with someone to talk to and keep you entertained while working out? Find a friend who will help hold you to your workout plans.

HEALTHY EATING

Do you ever think back to the food pyramid we learned about in elementary school? It starts with carbohydrates on the bottom level, followed by fruits and veggies, dairy and meat, and fats in the smallest portion. Now, as adults who do the grocery shopping for ourselves, it can be easy to forget all about the food pyramid. Is it even still relevant?

Over the years, the USDA has made slight updates to the chart, but the basic structure remains the same. And the overall goal is to make sure that Americans eat a variety of foods. Think about what you ate yesterday. Did you eat something from most categories?

If you did, you're off to a great start in eating healthy. If not, no worries. You've got some great things to look forward to when you make progress in this area. For starters, eating a healthy, balanced diet is one of the biggest factors in maintaining a healthy weight. And a healthy weight can help ward off risks for things like diabetes, high cholesterol, stroke, and overall body pain that can result from obesity.

Food also provides us with the energy we need to get through our days. Food is fuel, and what we put into our body has the ability to charge us up or wear us down. I always say, what you eat today is really for your body tomorrow. Diets that are high in greens and other veggies, as well as whole grains and healthy oils, can help us keep our energy high throughout the day, which can make us more productive. But those results aren't immediate like a sugar high. Try eating healthier than normal for a day and pay attention to how you feel, not just immediately after but the next day too.

Focus on eating things that either come from the earth or occur naturally. Any ingredients you can't pronounce are a sure sign of processed foods. Instead, try to focus on vegetables, preferably with a range of colors.

And don't forget about good old-fashioned water. Everything in your body, down to your cells, relies on water to function. The old rule of thumb has always been eight glasses a day, but the Mayo Clinic recommends around fifteen glasses for men and twelve for women.[8] And if you're exercising quite a bit or live in a warm climate, you may need even more.

All in all, there is a huge amount of information out there about what kinds of food are most healthy for you. One day, whole grains are in, and the next, they're out. Some diets recommend cutting out meat, others carbohydrates. One day, the morning shows tell us that a glass of wine a day is good for your heart, and then the next day, they tell us that it's bad. But while the health industry debates individual foods and ingredients, there are some things that they've come to a consensus about. Mainly, that's the power of vegetables and variety. So try some new recipes, incorporate as many fresh ingredients as you can, and pay attention to which foods make you *feel* best.

TIPS FOR EATING HEALTHIER

- ▸ **BUY A WATER BOTTLE.** Be sure to drink enough water throughout the day. Having a water bottle readily available will help you remember to keep drinking.

- ▸ **MEAL PREP.** Planning ahead is so important to getting in the habit of healthy eating. If junk food is readily available and there are no

---

8   https://www.mayoclinic.org/healthy-lifestyle/nutrition-and-healthy-eating/in-depth/water/art-20044256?pg=1

healthy options within arm's reach, you're more likely to go for the bad stuff. You're also more likely to go for healthy options if you do more cooking than eating out.

▸ **DON'T BUY PROCESSED FOODS. DON'T KEEP THEM IN THE HOUSE.** When you see a food that has ingredients you can't pronounce, steer clear. Processed foods rarely offer any nutritional value and are often high in sugar. If you want to learn more, there is no shortage of information out there on the effects of processed foods. But for now, trust me. You'll feel better without them.

▸ **SHOP AROUND THE OUTSIDE OF THE GROCERY STORE.** Grocery stores are designed strategically. Around the perimeter of the store, you'll find veggies, dairy, meat, and the bakery. On the interior aisles, you're more likely to find all the processed foods we're trying to avoid.

▸ **ASK YOURSELF, DID THIS COME FROM THE EARTH?** Just like the indecipherable ingredient list, consider where your food came from. If nothing in your meal came from the earth, like veggies or meat, consider looking up some healthier recipes.

▸ **SUBSCRIBE TO A HEALTHY RECIPE SITE, LIKE HEALTHYISH OR YOUR FAVORITE FOOD BLOGGER.** Make meal planning easier on yourself. Sign up for newsletters that will put healthy recipes right in your inbox.

▸ **KEEP A FOOD JOURNAL FOR A FEW DAYS.** A food journal is a great way to make yourself aware of mindless eating choices, like grabbing a donut at work or a piece of chocolate after dinner. If you're not careful, those little indulgences can add up.

SLEEP

Sleep is such an important aspect of our health that Ariana Huffington wrote an entire book on the topic. Top CEO's and industry leaders regularly talk about their reliance on sleep to put their best, most productive foot forward each day.

Of course, we also hear about the leader who wakes up at 3:00a.m. and gets more done before breakfast than the rest of us do all day, all while still going to bed at a normal hour. Our society loves the hustle. We often praise those who rarely take vacation, who are the first in and the last out of the office. The people who make us wonder, *How do they do it all?*

In striving to be our best selves, sleep is often the first sacrifice we make. If we wake up an hour earlier, we can make a case for that promotion or we can do some cleaning around the house before the kids get up. If we can just have a little more time, we can push a little harder. There's always more to do, but Arianna Huffington is right. When we sacrifice sleep just to cross one more thing off our to-do lists, we're taking a large step toward burnout.

When we miss out on sleep consistently, our overall productivity takes a hit. Our minds become fuzzy. We lose the will to keep up with workouts. We forget our "whys." In fact, research has told us that losing too much sleep can have the same effect as alcohol intoxication. Now, I'm not claiming there's anything wrong with imbibing from time to time after hours, but if you regularly showed up to work drunk, you'd lose your job. Why would you want to show up to work—or to most of your life—in a state that resembles it?

On the flip side of these side effects of sleep deprivation, those who do get the recommended amount of sleep (7–9 hours for adults per the National Sleep Foundation) are shown to have more positive outlooks. Everyone is different, so you may need more, or you may need less. But if you've spent any time around toddlers, you know that temper tantrums are often a sign that it's naptime. Well, as adults, we haven't changed all that much. When we're tired, we're way more likely to be cranky or angry.

Getting enough sleep also has a huge effect on memory. Asleep, our brains have a chance to process everything it remembers from the day before. And when we wake, we're more likely to remember those details more clearly.

And on top of all of that, there are also amazing benefits to your health itself. For starters, those who get solid sleep tend to have stronger immune systems than those who are sleep deprived, meaning they're less likely to catch colds or viruses. Additionally, several studies have shown that people who have been missing out on sleep for extended periods of time have greater risks for things like diabetes, heart attacks, and heart disease.

Those of you who work out often know that you shouldn't work the same muscle groups day in and day out. If your arms are sore from yesterday's workout, today you should focus on something else. All the microtears in your arm muscles from the day before need time to heal in order to properly build muscle. They need time to rest.

If you've been going and going, rest is a must. It will restore your mind and body. And, though it feels counterintuitive since you'll be spending more time unconscious (and therefore unable to work toward your goals), you will be more productive in your waking hours and be able to reach those goals more quickly.

HOW TO GET BETTER SLEEP

So now that I've convinced you of the importance of good, quality sleep, how do we get it? It's important to remember that in order to get restful sleep, we must start with a restful environment. Here are a few ideas for how to create just that.

1 **GIVE YOURSELF A BEDTIME.** Going to bed at a consistent time will help make getting a good night's sleep a habit. Set an alarm on your phone to remind you when to start getting ready for bed.

2 **PUT YOUR PHONE AWAY & AVOID ELECTRONICS.** Try to give yourself an hour away from screens before going to sleep. Scrolling through

your phone, answering emails, or watching TV right before bed can negatively affect your sleep.

3 **DO SOMETHING TO CALM YOUR MIND, LIKE GRATITUDE JOURNALING, MEDITATION, OR DEEP BREATHING.** Find something that relaxes you and prepares you for sleep. When you lie down for bed, you shouldn't feel stressed or anxious.

4 **KEEP YOUR ROOM CLEAN.** Those who keep clean bedrooms, with fresh sheets and made beds, feel better about going to sleep at night and report better sleep. Make your bedroom a tranquil space where you'll be excited to spend time before falling asleep.

5 **READ BEFORE BED.** Reading is one of the quickest ways to reduce stress, and it provides an excellent activity to replace your phone or TV. On top of that, what you choose to read may help you out in the Mental Pillar.

As you read, don't forget to keep picking a new challenge every day from the list for this chapter. Doing so will help get you in the habit of thinking about your health more often and keep the three spinning plates—physical activity, healthy eating, and sleep—going with minimal wobbling. But in order for the habit to stick, we need something powerful to drive us. We need meaning.

IDENTIFYING YOUR "WHY"

Despite all of the benefits to healthy living we just talked about, we don't always do things that are in our best interest. We eat unhealthy foods because they're convenient. We skip exercises because we're busy. We start restrictive diets, only to give up on them after a few months. Unhealthy choices are rampant in our society, and if all of the warnings of disease or the promises of health's benefits aren't enough to make us behave differently, what will be?

I hear from people all the time who tell me that they want to start eating better and living a healthier lifestyle. Last week, a friend asked me how I resist all the snacks and treats brought around. He told me that he was trying to lose some weight and wanted to eat healthier. An hour later, I walked past the kitchen in our office and saw him eating a cupcake.

I laughed and said, "You *just* told me you were trying to eat healthier. What are you doing, my man?"

"I just can't resist a cupcake," he laughed back.

Hearing that, my response was simply, "Your 'why' is not strong enough."

An important part of setting goals is taking the time to understand why you want to achieve them. Oftentimes, we confuse the result we're seeking with why we're doing it. For instance, before I started doing yoga, I had set a goal for myself to lose 15 pounds. When I went through the day, I didn't avoid sweets because I had the words "15 pounds" looming over me. Instead, I did it because I knew my "why" was to get off the plateau I'd found myself on. To push my physical fitness to the next level. Above all, to show up to my life fully for the people around me that matter most.

Do you remember the story about my sister running her first half-marathon? For many people, signing up for a race like that is prompted by a desire to prove that they can do it, that they can hit their goal. For Hanna, her "why" was to feel better. She'd gotten away from working out often, and she wanted to use the half-marathon as a way to help get her back on track. Not just physically, but mentally as well.

I talked with her last week, and even though the race was months ago, she hasn't stopped. She told me that running and working out have played a huge part in helping relieve stress and anxiety, and she wants to continue making exercising a lifelong commitment. That is someone connected to her "why."

Connecting your own "why" to the goals you set for yourself is so important. On days when you want to give up or reach for that cupcake, your "why" is what will sustain you. The results you're hoping to achieve won't. They're often so far in the future that it seems like you'll never see those results, so what's the point? Your "why" is what reminds you that progress is about baby steps. Your "why" is what gets you through the day-to-day.

Your "why" is also deeply personal and doesn't need to align with anyone else's. You may sign up for a race with your best friend, while having a completely different reason for running it. Whatever your goal, there are many things that may fuel it. Here are some common "whys."

> ‣ I want to [insert goal like running a half-marathon or holding a plank for two minutes] to prove to myself that I can do it.
>
> ‣ I want to cross something off my bucket list.
>
> ‣ I want to be more productive at work.
>
> ‣ I want to be healthier and lower my risk for disease.
>
> ‣ I want to be a little bit better than I was yesterday.
>
> ‣ I want to be an example to others that it is absolutely possible to achieve your goals and dreams when you set your mind to it.

When you identify the "why," it impacts all of your choices. This will be important for any goal you set for yourself, physical or otherwise. And as we continue through this book, you'll hear me say it again. Because understanding what drives you will help you establish your values. And when you begin to live in accordance with those values, you'll find happiness and fulfillment.

Let's take a few moments now for you to set a physical goal for yourself. What's the first thing that comes to mind? What have you been thinking about for a while?

The strongest goals are SMART (specific, measurable, achievable, relevant, and time oriented). Start with something you feel comfortable with. Does cutting out sugar for a month sound intimidating? Do it for a week. A day. Show yourself it's possible and build from there. Explore what works for you.

Write it down and go ahead and dog-ear this page. Don't worry, I don't mind. If that's not your thing, write down an inspirational quote and put the paper here as a bookmark. Do something so that you'll easily be able to access this page again.

_____

_____

_____

_____

Next, take some time to think about why you want to achieve that goal. The answer may not come to you right away, so take your time. Be honest with yourself. When you have it, write it down here.

_____

_____

_____

_____

Keep in mind that wanting to lose a few pounds so that other people will find you more attractive probably won't cut it. Why do *you* want it? For many of us, it's difficult to set physical goals without letting other people's perceptions of us or our own insecurities creep in. Other people can certainly play a role in helping us reach our physical goals, and they can play an even bigger role in our "whys" but only when framed in a positive light. A long-time smoker who wants to quit so that he can be there for his kids will probably have an easier time of it than if his "why" was simply that his wife didn't like the smell. Sometimes it's painful to admit, but allow yourself to get personal when figuring out your "why."

As you continue to pick daily challenges, think about picking ones that will help you achieve the goal you've set. And when you're tired or just don't want to do it, remember your "why." Keep it typed in your phone. Write it on a Post-it, and stick it to your bathroom mirror. Don't let your "why" fall to the wayside.

FINDING YOUR SUPPORT SYSTEM

I mentioned that other people can play a motivating role in helping us achieve our goals. Let's spend a little more time together in this chapter talking about how other people will play into your health goals.

We have to interact with many people every day. That fact is inevitable. Friends, colleagues, family—they all play a role in our lives and will also play one in our health journeys. How often has it happened that someone you've gone to dinner with encourages you to get something unhealthy off the menu or to have just one more drink with them? On the flip side, if you've run any sort of race, you may have had some friends on the sidelines cheering you along.

When it comes to health and fitness goals, the people around us tend to fall into one of two buckets: detractors and supporters. You're going to encounter both.

Detractors tend to be the cynics. When you tell them about a goal you have, they may scoff and tell you how terrible it sounds. They may even ask how long you think you'll be able to keep it up or tell you a story about their own past failure in something similar. In most cases, they don't mean any harm. Either they're just vocalizing the fact that meeting a goal is often hard or they don't understand your personal goal. Remember, everyone is different. So if giving up alcohol for a month sounds boring to them, they'll say it. You probably wouldn't get their goals either.

You can't always change a detractor into a more positive person. You can let them know that you'd appreciate their support and hope for the best, but if they don't change their attitude, then what? Turn that cynicism into fuel. Whenever someone tells you how much your goal sucks or talks about how unattainable it is, feel free to make it part of your goal to prove them wrong. Let that additional drive serve as a reminder that your goals stand apart from everyone else's. That your goals do not need to align with theirs. Remember, we are all different.

Sometimes you may find people, usually friends, whose cynicism doesn't seem so innocuous. They go out of their way to tempt you into breaking your commitment to yourself. Going back to the example of giving up drinking, maybe they buy you a drink without asking or keep pushing for you to go out with them. Before getting too upset, take a second to put yourself in their shoes. Has your new goal changed the dynamic of your relationship? Is it just that your normal drinking buddy is upset that you're spending less time together?

Now, those situations aren't a reason to give up a goal or a lifestyle shift, but it does help to give you some perspective. Invite that friend to do something else that doesn't interfere with your goals. Relationships are so important in helping us become the people we want to be, so the more you are able to turn detracting friends into supportive friends, the better. Unfortunately, it doesn't always go that way. If a friendship can't evolve, then it may not be worth preserving. If the goal is to live in accordance with your values, and that friendship will constantly stand in the way of it, it will only be a long-term struggle for you to reach your goals. And the more your values grow apart, the harder it will be for you to support that friend in return.

So when times get tough, turn instead to the people who will lift you up, those glorious humans who can always brighten your spirits. When you need a pep talk, go to your supportive friends and family. Find a walking buddy who will help hold you accountable. Join a gym full of people who inspire you. Let their positive energy provide another kind of fuel for you as you work toward your goals. They will be the people who help carry you through the challenges coming up in the coming Pillars, too. So be grateful to them.

The people around us hold enormous power in our lives. As we've talked about, some may bring us down. But I think you'll find that most people do their best to lift us up. The people who love you *want* you to be happy. Don't you feel the same for the people you love? Let them in on this journey. Tell them about your goals. You'll be surprised how liberating and reassuring it can be.

And don't forget that you've got your own community right here. The AlwaysSmilin community was built to spread positive vibes to those who need it. We are here for you. You are never alone in your journey toward a happier life. So let's keep going together.

Before we head into the next chapter, let's quickly take stock of your progress so far. Have you completed some of the daily challenges? How have they made you feel? Did you enjoy any more than others? Are you feeling more productive already?

As we switch gears into the Mental Pillar, try to keep up with your physical improvement. Get some sleep, eat your veggies, and keep moving. Take it slow, and enjoy the process. Set new, achievable goals for yourself and keep checking them off. By keeping up with your physical health, your increased energy and more positive attitude will help propel you through the next chapter—and, of course, your life.

Are you ready to do some mental work? Of course you are! Let's get going.

CHAPTER 4

THE MENTAL PILLAR

"You gain strength, courage, and confidence by every
experience in which you really stop to look fear in the face.
You must do the thing you think you cannot do."

—ELEANOR ROOSEVELT

WHEN YOU THINK about the Navy SEALs, what comes to mind?

You might think of men in the middle of a combat zone in the Middle East. Maybe it's their faces painted in camouflage, as they wade through mud and carry big guns. Or maybe they're jumping out of helicopters into freezing waters. You could think of all the movie depictions you've seen and how SEALs are always portrayed as the best of the best. The toughest of the tough. The most elite of the elite.

Chances are qualities like strength, grit, and perseverance also come to mind. After all, they have to make it through the most grueling training process the U.S. military has to offer in order to call themselves SEALs. According to the Navy, "SEAL training has been described as brutal, preparing you for the extreme physical and mental challenges of SEAL missions."

In one week of training alone, appropriately called "Hell Week," nearly three quarters of trainees call it quits. So what separates the remaining SEALs from the pack? There are lots of answers to this question, but one of the most commonly repeated is mental toughness. They don't let their minds tell them they can't do it.

There's a popular story about a former Navy SEAL who lived with an executive for a month to help him do exactly what we're trying to do— get off of autopilot.[9] The former SEAL pushed his new roommate to his limits and introduced the "40% rule" to him, which says that when your mind is telling you you're done, you're only 40% of the way to your limit. To prove it, the SEAL pushed his new apprentice to do dozens more pull-ups than he ever thought possible. And he kept pushing the executive past his perceived limits, day after day.

The same philosophy often applies to long-distance runners, who may hit a wall late in the race but ultimately push through it to cross the finish line.

And I'm sure you can think of something you've done that fits that description, too. Is there a time when you surprised yourself with what you were able to accomplish? Maybe you had a deadline coming up and didn't think you'd be able to hit it. But you pushed through. Maybe you got distracted by your favorite song and realized you'd done double the push-ups you set out to do.

We can all point to times when we needed to push past what we thought possible, and we can point to times when we gave up because we got discouraged. The difference between accomplishing a goal and failing to meet it is rarely ability. More often than not, it's our mental state that determines our fate.

So in this chapter, we're going to focus on exactly that—our mental state. How do we improve it? How do we *control* it? How do we deal with

---

9   https://thehustle.co/40-percent-rule-navy-seal-secret-mental-toughness

all the things that are thrown at us in a given day? The Emotional Pillar is up next, and these two tend to bleed into one another quite a bit. For instance, if we get upset over a rude email at work, our emotions are definitely in play. But it's by training our mental state to get out of its old habits that helps keep those emotions from spiraling. In other words, this chapter is prep work for the next one, and it will help you through the Spiritual and Professional Pillars, too.

So what exactly do I mean when I talk about our mental state? Is it just our ability to get through tough things, sort of like the Navy SEALs? Absolutely! But that's not the whole story.

The Mental Pillar can be broken down into two parts: mental strength and mental curiosity. When we talk about the SEALs and overcoming negative emotions, we're often talking about mental strength, or the ability to create a positive state of mind despite outside forces. Mental curiosity, on the other hand, is about understanding other people, other cultures, and other ideas to help you identify what's important to you in life. In order to succeed at your personal goals, you'll need to practice both.

Before we talk about what you can do to improve in each area, let's first spend a few moments talking about why they matter.

THE NEED FOR MENTAL CURIOSITY

If I walked up to you on the street and asked you, right now, to tell me your top three values in life, do you think you'd be able to? I know many people, thoughtful and deliberate people, who would sputter and look at me with a blank stare if I did that. Thinking about what drives us and what we stand for isn't something we can do at the drop of a hat. It requires thought and exploration. It requires time. And more than anything, it requires curiosity.

Let's back up for a second and say that instead I asked you to tell me your favorite ice cream flavor. Much easier, right? Mine would be cookies and cream, no question. You might say mint chocolate chip or pistachio or even good old-fashioned vanilla. But if vanilla ice cream was the only flavor you had *ever* tried, would you feel comfortable calling it your favorite? There's so much out there that you haven't sampled yet. How can you know for sure?

I bring up that scenario for a simple reason. Every day we are able to make decisions about what we like and what we dislike, what's important to us and what's not, without knowing everything there is to know about a topic. We don't need to try every last ice cream flavor, down to lavender honey or berry goat cheese, to have a favorite. Besides, I already mentioned that the best is cookies and cream.

That said, we do need to do some sampling. We need to be curious about what else is out there. Later, when we really do write down our values, it's important to know how other people live and why they value different things in order to feel confident in your own direction. In other words, we need to try someone else's favorite ice cream, walk in their shoes for a moment. By doing so, it's my hope that you will be able to identify your values and your passions—and that you'll go on to pursue those passions with all your might.

There are a few added benefits to mental curiosity beyond helping you identify your own values. First, by learning more about other people and ideas, you will be better equipped to avoid judgement. I'm not saying that you need to accept all other ideas as your own, but if you come across someone who thinks differently, you'll be slower to judge them for it. Hopefully you'll respond instead with empathy, and with that your relationships will deepen.

Next, you'll be able to practice gratitude. Do you remember when we talked about the importance of gratitude in your journey toward happiness and how stillness can help you find it? Understanding more about the world and your place in it will provide you with another route to gratitude. It's so easy to get caught up in the everyday annoyances of our lives (that rude email at work, for example) and forget how easy we have it compared to so many others. I've certainly been there before. But reading more, talking to new people, and staying curious have helped me to snap out of those moments more quickly.

Above all, if your goal for picking up this book was to lead a better life, it begins by thinking about life differently. Something isn't working now, and change is the only path toward a happier life. I've talked before about going into this book and into the daily challenges with an open mind. This is how you help open your mind to new ideas. It starts with exposure to them.

And speaking of daily challenges, if you haven't already, switch over to picking a few from the Mental Pillar. At the end of the book, we'll create a month's worth of challenges tailored to you from each Pillar, but as you read, just focus on the Pillar at hand.

THE POWER OF MENTAL STRENGTH

When I think about why mental strength matters, I think of an old quote I love that reads:

"Watch your thoughts, they become words;
watch your words, they become actions;
watch your actions, they become habits;
watch your habits, they become character;
watch your character, it becomes your destiny."

This is *everything* we've been talking about so far. It's about breaking down "destiny" (or fulfillment in our case) into smaller and smaller pieces. And it all starts with thoughts. Mental strength isn't important so that you can make it through Navy SEAL Hell Week—though you would need it if you chose this route! It's important so that you can have greater control over your own life and happiness.

Those who are able to control their thoughts and mindsets are more likely to achieve their goals because they can visualize themselves doing it. They don't let negative thoughts creep in and ruin their motivation. Think about it this way: Every time you are able to push out a negative thought, you are achieving a small goal. You're already one step closer to your larger goal. Mental strength can start small with greater awareness of your mindset and build into an understanding that you are capable of achieving much more.

On that note, one thing that I've heard over and over again is that people don't think they have the power to choose positivity. There are too many things that happen to them that affect the emotions they feel. In the Emotional Pillar chapter, we'll talk in more detail about how you can work through negative emotions and tough periods in your life, and mental strength will play a huge role in that process. For now, think of mental strength as the ability to control your thoughts. When we get to the Emotional Pillar, we'll talk more about the way controlling your thoughts can, in turn, help you control your emotions.

But I'm getting ahead of myself here. The main reason mental strength matters is because of the snowball effect it can have. It's a shorter jump than you might think from "thoughts" to "destiny," and it's my hope that you'll start this journey off with the right frame of mind so that you can achieve everything you hope to.

Think back to the different scenarios we explored in Chapter 1 about moving to a new city. Whether or not we found happiness in our new lives relied very little on the circumstances presented. In fact, in that example, all the outside forces remained exactly the same. The only difference was in the mindset applied to the move. The belief that we would be okay.

But what if the circumstances do change? What if there are forces beyond our control that get in the way of controlling our thoughts?

THE INS AND OUTS OF INTERNAL AND EXTERNAL FORCES

Circumstances pop up everyday that have the potential to interfere with our goals and happiness, and they often fall into one of two categories: internal forces or external forces. Internal forces, like doubt or anger, challenge our mental curiosity by allowing us to rely on our existing biases and habits. External forces, on the other hand, challenge our mental strength and make it feel impossible to gain control of our thoughts again. They're things beyond our control, like rude drivers on our morning commute.

Unfortunately, there's no avoiding these forces altogether. If life is like a river, some metaphorical rocks and boulders are inevitable. Unless we live in solitary confinement, things will pop up that will have the potential to detract from our happiness. And once you've dealt with one—once you've successfully maneuvered around a boulder—there's another one on the horizon. And that's OK.

Never fear, my friends. **No matter how your life evolves and what things are thrown at you, you are in complete control of one absolutely pivotal thing: how you react to them.**

Think of mental curiosity and mental strength as your paddles. Practicing them will help you to control how you react to things and to successfully steer yourself through rough waters. Let's spend some time now talking about what the heck these internal and external forces are and then about how you can build up your mental curiosity and strength to combat them. It'll be like rowing practice. Let's embark.

INTERNAL FORCES: A TEST OF YOUR CURIOSITY

Internal forces are a tricky business because they're completely invisible. No one else in your life knows when you're experiencing them, and only you can stop them from interfering with your happiness.

Tell me if this situation sounds familiar. You sit down at your desk in the morning in a great mood. You open your email, and the first email that you read is from an upset client. Now, they're not just expressing slight disappointment. They're pissed off, and they're *rude*.

For many of us, our first thought would be, *Well, my day is ruined.*

And that seems totally justified, right? Someone being disproportionately angry and rude to you, likely for things that were out of your control anyways, can be seriously upsetting.

So when a coworker sees you in the kitchen later and asks you how your day is going, you may launch into the whole story or you may grunt and walk away. Either way, when these things happen, it becomes apparent to the people around you very quickly that something is up.

On the surface, it may seem like this situation was triggered by an external force, the email. After all, anyone could read the email. Anyone could see that this was the result of someone else's original action. But there's another, more subtle force at play here: the feeling of justified anger.

The internal force here is the split second it took for you to read the email and think, *I deserve to feel angry.* And that instant kicked off a chain of events that could have included anything from complaining about the situation to colleagues or sending a less-than-ideal response to perhaps even saying something rude to your spouse or partner in frustration.

In short, internal forces are the thoughts we have that justify our behaviors.

If you're trying to lose weight but can't resist office treats, the internal force may be a feeling that you deserve a reward for eating well all day or that a few pieces can't *really* be that bad. If you need to have a productive day at work, an internal force may be focusing on how tired you feel and doubting your ability to get much done.

Internal forces can also include personal biases that you have. Maybe you choose not to hold the door open for someone because you make a split-second judgment about them based on their appearance or clothing.

Internal forces can be positive, too. If you notice something nice about someone else, an internal force may tell you to voice your compliment, rather than keep it to yourself. What we're going for here is to learn to turn negative thoughts into positive ones like this.

Negative internal forces can be sparked by anything, but the common thread is that there is an instantaneous assumption that's made that tells us we either can't or don't need to act in a way that lines up with our values. They're the excuses we tell ourselves to do what feels easier or better in the moment.

And why do those things feel easier and better? Why does an angry response to the email feel easier, or more natural, to us than a calm response that doesn't interfere with the rest of our day? Just think about the fallout from that single email. There's no way that that route, which included feeling upset all day and potentially taking it out on your spouse, is easier than letting go of the anger and moving on.

It feels easier simply because the response has become a habit. Over time, you've conditioned yourself to become angry at such situations. You've seen other people react that way when it happens to them. And so, even though you're in the middle of a quest to be happy, when something similar pops up, you react how you always have—and often, the way that has been modeled for you by others.

We've already spent a lot of time talking about habits and how difficult they are to break, but so far we've mostly been talking about physical habits. Things that we want to *do* or stop *doing*. There's action involved.

So how do we change habits as they relate to our thoughts? How do we make sure that we replace those negative forces with positive ones?

NAVIGATING INTERNAL FORCES

You guessed it. We're going to talk more about mental curiosity here.

It makes sense that the key to combating our mental biases and negative habits lies in expanding our minds. After all, the mind is where all of this action is happening. Our thoughts are what compel us to act in certain undesirable ways, and our thoughts can stop us from that behavior, too.

It's like an imaginary battle happening between Past You and Future You in your head. Future You wants you to act in a way that lines up with your values, while Past You wants you to keep behaving how you always have. Past You wants you to say things like, "Why should I change?" or, "This is just who I am."

But the major downside of this imaginary battle is that, when Past You wins, it can have some very real results for both you and all the other people in your life (like the spouse or partner you took your anger out on).

And when you fail to hold the door open for someone based on how they look, you make an assumption about that person, which can be downright hurtful. Now, we all know what they say happens when you assume, and "they" are spot on. The beauty of life lies in the uniqueness we each possess and in what we are able to share with one another.

Above all, we have to remember that what got us to this point in our lives won't get us to the next level. We must think and act differently.

The more we learn from others, the more we can replace assumptions with facts and differing perspectives that can help us get to that next level. There is so much that we are able to learn from one another, and in doing so, we are able to explore some of the deepest facets of life.

On top of that, the more you fill your mind with examples of people who have succeeded in the areas you hope to, the more you condition your mind to recognize its own potential. The more you are able to emulate those people. The more routes to success you unlock. The more you understand your purpose in life.

Learning about different ideas and people looks different to everyone. If you were to tell me to go learn everything I could about a topic, my first instinct would be to talk to as many people as I could. Someone else may check out every book on the topic at the library. There's no right way to learn, but I am going to share some strategies with you to spark your mental curiosity. Hopefully, you will begin to challenge your own assumptions, look to other people for new perspectives, and distill what you learn into values that are important to you.

STEP 1: YOU DON'T KNOW WHAT YOU DON'T KNOW

Cultivating your mental curiosity comes, first and foremost, by establishing a love of learning. So go ahead and throw out any preconceived notions you have about being a nerd. Our culture loves to poke fun at intelligent, learned people, and I just can't wrap my head around why. Lifelong learning can unlock so many new opportunities, many you may not have known anything about otherwise. So kudos to you for picking up this book!

Have you ever played trivia with friends? There's usually one person on every team that knows the answers to the most random questions. Everyone at the table turns to look at them in disbelief when they confidently give their answer. They think, *How on Earth do you know that?*

Chances are that person genuinely enjoys learning new things. They pick up books on topics they know little about. They may read the paper every day or listen to podcasts on a variety of topics. They are energized by understanding more about the world.

People like your trivia buddy help demonstrate the sheer volume of information in the world. And the hard truth is that, in your current bubble, you may not realize how much you're missing out on knowing. You may not know the extent to which you could be further connecting with your own life.

Developing mental curiosity will help expose you to new ideas that you didn't even know you wanted to learn. So how do you do it? Here are a few ideas:

- **READ.** I encourage you to try to read something every single day. Pick out books from a variety of genres. Go to a different news site or blog than you normally do. Make sure that what you read comes from writers of many backgrounds and opinions. We often get our news from social media, so take note of who you are following and what kind of information they share. Try following some different news accounts or influencers, or make it a point to stay off social media entirely for a few days. Force yourself to find new ways to stay informed.

- **LISTEN.** This is truly a golden age for podcasts. And the beautiful thing about them is that they are totally free. You can learn about nearly anything, straight from the mouths of experts. Podcasts are excellent watercooler conversation starters. So if you don't know what to listen to first, ask for a recommendation. And if you want to go deeper into one topic, give audiobooks a try. They're the perfect remedy for a long commute.

- **WATCH.** I put this last because television can quickly turn into a rabbit hole. You can sit down on the couch, prop your feet up, and sail through five hours of *Friends* reruns seemingly at the blink of an eye. But if TV and movies are your thing, switch it up. Make it a goal to not watch something you've seen before. Try out a documentary. Watch a foreign film or a historical drama. Or go online and check out some TED Talks or YouTube videos by people you admire. Give something a chance you normally wouldn't.

So Step 1 to building up your mental curiosity comes through the media you consume, but Step 2 is arguably more important.

STEP 2: YOUR NETWORK IS YOUR NET WORTH

Are you tired of hearing me say it yet? The people you surround yourself with can have an enormous impact on you and your happiness.

Your mental curiosity is no different. Do your best to surround yourself with interesting people who will challenge your ideas and assumptions. This often means spending time with people who are very different from you. Maybe that includes people who have an extreme drive for life, people who have a more positive outlook on things, or people who simply come from a different background.

A common complaint I hear about this idea is that your job or your neighborhood doesn't have much diversity. How can you make friends with people outside your immediate circle?

For starters, there are so many more ways to get to know people in your community than just meeting friends through work. (Though I'll admit, it is often the easiest method.) Sign up for a volunteer activity. Join a sports league or go to a few meetups. Plan a dinner or a happy hour and ask each friend to bring someone new. Start a book club. The possibilities for breaking out of your own bubble are endless, but I do understand that it can be scary.

So start slow. Start with your existing network. I'm willing to bet that some of your acquaintances, and maybe even some of your close friends, have some interesting life experiences you haven't heard about yet. Try to start up conversations that go a little deeper with those people. Ask them questions and genuinely try to get to know them better.

We're all guilty of repeating the same boring conversation that goes something like this:

ME: How have you been, man?

YOU: Oh, good. Good. Busy! But no complaints. How about you?

ME: Pretty much the same. Life has been crazy lately.

YOU: Yeah.

ME: Yeah.

Instead, start probing a little deeper with the people in your network. Ask them meaningful questions about their lives. Rather than looking for an opportunity to interject with your own stories, listen deeply to what they have to say. I'm willing to bet that when you get past this kind of boring, surface-level conversation, you'll learn something new. You'll also find the conversation much more interesting, which will help you get in the habit of seeking out these kinds of conversations in the future.

If it feels a little weird at first, make it a game. Try to learn one new thing about every person you talk to for a day, a week, a month, and so on. And remember, it only feels weird because you made it a habit not to ask these kinds of questions. Push past it, and the weirdness will disappear.

At this point, you're learning more both from the media you consume and from the people in your life. So now it's time to pay it forward. Let's move on to Step 3.

STEP 3: GIVE BACK

Volunteering and giving back to your community is not only a great way to meet more people, but it's also a great way expand your mind. By volunteering your time and energy, you will inevitably learn more about the causes you support and, more importantly, about the people you're helping.

I can tell you without a doubt that in my time as a Big Brothers Big Sisters volunteer, I have learned just as much from my Little Brother as he has from me. When I ran the marathon and raised money for cancer research, I learned more about cancer treatment options and what patients need when going through treatment. In doing so, I felt a great amount of empathy for what they were going through.

Volunteerism is the ultimate way to become a more empathetic person because you are connecting directly with someone else's vulnerability. It provides an enormous opportunity for us, as I mentioned in Step 3, to meet people who think differently than we do. People who worry about different things than we do.

And it's through volunteering that we can gain perspective when internal forces start to pop up. When you begin to doubt your abilities or question the possibility of achieving your goals, you will be more comfortable in the practice of giving yourself grace. You'll forgive yourself when you fall short and move forward anyway.

All too often, we feel that our negative emotions or thoughts are justified by what the world throws at us. The truth is that, no matter what is thrown your way, someone else has faced worse. When you give freely of your time and energy, you will have a better understanding of the range of human conditions. You will be able to put your own justifications for anger or jealousy or any unwanted behavior into the context of a much larger framework.

Here are a few ideas to get you started:

▸ **ASK AROUND.** If you're not sure where you'd like to start volunteering, ask your friends what they do. Talk to coworkers. Get some suggestions of places that need a volunteer's time, not just money.

▸ **FOLLOW YOUR PASSIONS.** Do you already have a cause that you're passionate about? Maybe you read a lot about a particular topic but haven't gotten involved in it yet. Research organizations that focus on areas you're already interested in.

▸ **FUNDRAISE.** Donating money to causes you care about can make a huge impact, but if you can't afford to donate large sums, consider fundraising efforts. Ask people to make donations in lieu of birthday gifts or a wedding registry. Run a race on a fundraising team. Raising money often means that you need to talk about the cause with other people, meaning you need to learn a great deal about it first. You're also doing more good by exposing other people to a valuable cause that they may want to support, too.

STEP 4: GET UNCOMFORTABLE

I understand that pushing yourself to grow your mental curiosity isn't always a comfortable endeavor. I'm willing to wager that you may have even cringed at the idea of joining a book club or leading a fundraiser. We all have our comfort zones, and meeting people who challenge our ideas often lies well outside of them. But doing so is crucial for growing your mental curiosity because, once you start to expand your horizons, you will want to keep doing it. You'll see how much more the world has to offer. Remember this. You can't spell challenge, without change. So, being uncomfortable is natural in this process if you are changing.

My advice for getting started? Follow the Nike tagline's advice and *Just Do It.*

I'm not saying you need to sign up to be on the board of a charity right away or that you need to invite someone you barely know away for a weekend retreat to bond. Use your daily challenges to start small. Bit by bit, force yourself out of your comfort zone. Eventually, your comfort zone will widen in response.

Over time, something amazing will happen. You'll notice that your mind may naturally shift to a more positive outlook. In times of doubt or frustration, the little angel on your shoulder will be a bit louder than the devil.

When you think, *I deserve that cupcake for eating so well today*, you'll remember the article you read on the addictive qualities of processed sugar and how hard it will be for you to get back on track. Instead, you'll reward yourself by taking a walk outside or calling a friend.

When you're feeling tired and your hopes for a productive day at work are ruined, you'll think of your friend who is the most productive person you know, despite having a newborn in the house and a side hustle.

When you don't want to hold the door open for the person behind you, you'll think about the people at the soup kitchen you served and recognize that you have no idea what that person has gone through. They may need a kind gesture.

However you hope to grow, whether you want to be more mindful to others or just want to lose some weight, mental curiosity will help you to change your thoughts. And when you make the right decision in those split-second moments, it can have positive ripple effects throughout your entire day and beyond.

EXTERNAL FORCES: A TEST OF YOUR MENTAL STRENGTH

If internal forces are completely invisible, happening only in our minds, external forces live in the world at large. They are the events we go through every day that we have no control over. They're the actions of people we interact with. In short, they're the byproduct of needing to engage with the world around us, instead of living in isolation. And as we walk through life, we make hundreds of decisions a day, usually about how to react to external forces like:

- The bus that runs late one morning
- The computer that crashes
- The snow or rain that falls on you
- The person who bumps you with their cart at the grocery store

Or:

- The lucky penny you find on the street
- The card your coworkers sign for your birthday
- The stranger who compliments your outfit
- The cotton candy sunset on your camping trip

Being more mentally curious will help you to think through your reactions to any one of the above situations, especially the negative ones. But being mentally strong is the other half of the equation. Mental strength is what will drive change for you over time. It's one thing to make one split-second decision that aligns with your values. It's another thing entirely to make hundreds of decisions in a row that do.

Change begins with our thoughts (internal) but ultimately depends on our actions (external) to truly take hold. External forces are all around us, but it isn't the simple fact that they exist that trips us up on our journey to happiness. It's the constant barrage of them.

Let's go back to the Navy SEALs for a moment. During training, they have to make it through an underwater exercise where the instructors simulate an attack on the trainees. For many, it's one of the most terrifying drills, but that one drill isn't the reason so many fail. They fail because that drill was one of many that day, and it was performed after they were only allowed a few hours of sleep. It's one thing after another that, each taken alone, would be enough to scare most of us out of training. But taken all together? That's why only the mentally toughest make it through.

How many times have you felt like your day snowballed out of your control because of external forces? The bus had to be late on the morning it snowed. When you finally got to work, your computer wouldn't turn on. And on top of all that, someone had the audacity to bump you with their cart at the grocery store. Cue the glass of wine when you get home, cancel the plans you'd made, and turn on some mindless TV instead. Maybe tomorrow you'll wake up in a better mood.

We have *all* been there.

We have all experienced bad days when it feels like the whole world is out to get us. And most of us have experienced even worse, like losing a job or learning that a loved one has passed away. Practicing mental strength on the days when the worst thing to happen is someone stealing your great parking spot will help you get through the tougher times. Because, the truth is, when you lose a job, you don't wake up the next morning in a better mood. It takes time—and work—to pull yourself out of that kind of negative headspace.

Mental strength is the key to stopping a string of external forces from bringing you down. It's also the key to not letting those same external forces get in the way of your goals or the life you want to create. When you cancel your plans to watch Netflix instead, how much further are you setting yourself back in your goals? What progress could you have made, had you not let those external forces bring you down?

External forces, like internal ones, are a part of life. They are inevitable. So instead of bowing to them on particularly bad days, how about we learn to work through them instead? By doing so, we're ensuring that no matter what life throws at us, we can handle it.

COMBATING EXTERNAL FORCES

Mentally tough people don't get there overnight. Mental strength, like physical strength, requires training. Just like going to the gym and lifting weights, it's important that you build up your mental strength over time.

The end goal is that when things that are outside of your control happen, you will have developed a thicker skin to help you deal with it. By developing your mental curiosity, you will have trained your mind not to make assumptions or doubt yourself in a way that interferes with your values. And by developing strength, you will be telling the outside world that anything it throws at you will roll off your back and that you'll stay focused on achieving your goals.

No external force can bring you down for long.

Like any goal that takes time, the key to tackling it is to break it into its smaller parts and move piece by piece. Since there is no shortage of external forces for you to deal with on a daily basis, you'll get plenty of practice. How lucky! You can move as quickly or as slowly through the following exercises as you want. For now, let's start with one of the simplest ways to continuously shift your mindset.

STEP 1: PRACTICE SMILING

There's a reason I named our company AlwaysSmilin. Not only does a smile help to cheer up the people around you, spreading your positive vibes to them as a result, but it also has the same effect on you.

Science has proven that when we smile, we feel happier. Our mood is instantly boosted. And with that improved mood, we're more productive. We may even be healthier.[10]

So how does this relate to dealing with external forces? This is one of the easiest ways to reset your mind in times of stress. When you feel yourself becoming overwhelmed by something you can't control, take a few deep breaths, find something to help you crack a smile, and wait a few minutes before responding.

---

10   https://www.nbcnews.com/better/health/
     smiling-can-trick-your-brain-happiness-boost-your-health-ncna822591

And if you're not sure what to smile about, remember that you have so much to be grateful for in your life. Ask yourself what you are most grateful for at that moment, or think about the person who means the most to you. Chances are a smile will make its way to your face after that.

Here's how to start smiling more:

▸ **START A MORNING ROUTINE.** Make it a goal to smile genuinely about something within the first hour of your day. Save your phone alarm as a funny message to yourself or an encouraging quote. Find time to laugh with your partner. Write in a gratitude journal. Whatever you need to do to kick your day off on the right foot.

▸ **STOP SAYING "THAT'S FUNNY."** When you find something funny, don't comment on it. *Laugh.* Allow yourself to enjoy the positive moments of your day more fully.

▸ **SMILE ALONE.** No one likes being told they should smile more, so don't do it for anyone else. Do it for yourself. When you read a heartwarming news article on your computer, smile. When you read a funny joke on Twitter, laugh. Smiling in isolation feels really awkward at first, but when you're able to do so alone without any discomfort, you can bet you'll be smiling more in the company of others.

▸ **BE AWARE OF YOUR "RESTING FACE."** When you're staring at your computer or listening to a presentation, does your face naturally settle into a scowl? Bring some awareness to your resting face and take notice when you start to furrow your brows or purse your lips. When you find yourself doing it, try to relax the muscles in your face instead and you'll feel a slight, but immediate, change in mood. And over time, you'll train yourself to put forward more positive, open facial expressions.

Smiling more is a relatively easy one. You just need to remember to do it. So leave little reminders for yourself or set a daily goal to smile at least 10 times. The next step will be much easier to achieve if you're already in the habit of smiling often.

STEP 2: VISUALIZE SUCCESS

We've all heard the sports joke, "Be the ball." It's all about visualizing yourself as the ball and imagining exactly where it will go. By doing so, theoretically you'll be able to make it happen. Though that quote originally came to us courtesy of *Caddyshack*, there is actually some merit to it.

When Michael Phelps prepares for a race, he visualizes every possible outcome. He thinks through the race step-by-step, imagining everything in the pool and thinking about where he should be at each mental checkpoint. He thinks through scenarios like what would happen if he fell behind in the first lap.

His coach claims that Michael's ability to visualize himself winning is one of the reasons he's so successful. When he finally gets in the pool on race day, he knows exactly what he needs to do, and he's practiced doing it dozens of times.[11]

No matter what your goal is, visualizing yourself achieving it will help you get there. If your goal is a happier life, work to create a clear picture of what that life looks like. (Side note: If you don't know what that looks like quite yet, that's okay. We'll get there by the end of this book.) If you're hoping for a promotion, visualize yourself getting it. What steps did you need to take? What would you do if your boss told you it wasn't in the budget? What if you make a mistake in your work before the big ask? How will you handle it?

When you have a clear vision of what you want and how to get it, you will be better able to bob and weave around any external forces that

---

11 https://www.forbes.com/sites/carminegallo/2016/05/24/3-daily-habits-of-peak-performers-according-to-michael-phelps-coach/#6f848275102c

come up. In other words, keep your eye on the prize, and you'll find a way to get it.

These are a few ideas to help you visualize your success:

‣ **THINK ABOUT IT DAILY.** When you have an image of success in your mind, conjure it up often. Try to think of different scenarios for getting there, as well as potential roadblocks.

‣ **WRITE IT DOWN.** What exactly does success look like? List out the different characteristics of it. If it's a promotion, what new duties do you want? What kind of salary? Get crystal clear on what you're going after.

‣ **SET MANAGEABLE GOALS.** No matter what your major goal is, you'll need to break it into baby steps. Don't try to tackle everything in one day. Visualize each step of the process and tackle them one by one. And make 100% sure that every step is in line with your personal values.

‣ **SAY IT OUT LOUD.** Start by saying it to a mirror and build your way up to telling someone else who will help you support that vision. Pick someone that will be stoked by your amazing vision and may even challenge you to think bigger.

Mental visualization is one of the most important steps in building up mental strength. But even with a clear goal in sight, external forces can throw us off. So you may need the wisdom of others to help get you back on track.

STEP 3: FIND POSITIVE AFFIRMATIONS

Have you given motivational quotes a chance yet? You know what I'm talking about. I'm talking about those quote images that are all over Instagram and Pinterest. If you haven't, I think you'll be surprised by the power they can have in keeping your mind in a positive state. When I read a motivational quote by someone I admire, I often find instant clarity. The right quote at the right time can change my whole day.

Think about the last time someone motivated you. Maybe it was a coach or a mentor who pushed you in the right direction. When someone else has faith in you and your abilities, you start to believe it yourself.

Motivational quotes (cheesy as some may consider them) work the same way. According to a recent *Fast Company* article, looking at motivational quotes is a like "implicit coaching."[12] Only, instead of relying on a mentor or coach for positive words, you supply them yourself through positive quotes.

According to the same article, there are a few hallmarks to a good quote, including that it be memorable. So rhyming or parallel speech patterns tend to stand out to us.

Another big component is that they come from those who have achieved results we admire. Famous writers, thinkers, business leaders, or politicians tend to supply some of the most popular quotes, which makes sense. Of course we're more likely to take the advice of someone we look up to, someone whose success we hope to replicate.

So before you knock them, give them a try. When an external force gets in your way, a positive quote may be just what you need to help you refocus on your goals and to believe that you can achieve them.

Here's where you'll find them:

▸ **SOCIAL MEDIA.** Positive quotes are all over social media, especially on Instagram and Pinterest. If you let it, social media can be a welcoming community for you. Follow accounts that make you feel good (AlwaysSmilin is always posting positive quotes) and unfollow or hide those that don't.

---

12 https://www.fastcompany.com/3051432/why-inspirational-quotes-motivate-us

▸ **START WITH PEOPLE YOU ADMIRE.** If you don't want to go down the social media route, good ole Google will be your best friend. Think about someone you admire and look for quotes by them. You could also write down some wise words from your personal mentor. Print them out or type them in your phone's notes. Keep it handy for when you need someone to look up to.

STEP 4: PRACTICE

So you see, mental strength is not so difficult to achieve, is it? Smile more, visualize your goals, and read some inspirational quotes—is that really all?

Those simple tips could certainly get you through the average day. They'd help you become more productive and positive, and you'd be able to move past any of the everyday annoyances that could usually throw you off track.

That said, the other element needed to truly consider yourself mentally strong is time. **I believe that you can teach yourself how to feel joy in your bones, but it needs to be conditioned in you to last.**

Remember, mental strength is not about making one decision that lines up with your values. It's about making sure that *all* of your decisions line up with your values and support your goals. Getting to that point requires practice. It requires that you be tested from time to time. Just as important, it requires that you fail from time to time.

Over time, the more you train your mind, the stronger it will become. I can't stress enough that striving for happiness and fulfillment is a lifelong process. You can always count on external forces to change over time and throw you more than you *think* you can handle. But if your ability to channel a positive mindset remains constant through continual practice, there is nothing you can't overcome. There is nothing you can't achieve.

KNOW YOUR TRIGGERS

Before we move on, I have a final exercise for you. I believe it's important to identify your particular areas of mental weakness so that you can fight against them. In a given day, what tends to pull you away from your goals the most? Is it internal forces, like doubt or assumptions? Or is it all the stuff you can't control?

By bringing awareness to your specific triggers, you'll be more likely to respond differently the next time they come up.

Think about your day today, and write down every negative emotion you experienced. Were you annoyed, angry, doubtful? What triggered these emotions?

EMOTION

Ex. Annoyance

TRIGGER (INTERNAL / EXTERNAL FORCE)

Dirty laundry on the floor at home

It probably didn't feel too great to relive those moments from your day, did it? So let's do the opposite now. **Write down the positive emotions you felt today, and think about what triggered them. What makes you smile?**

EMOTION	**TRIGGER (INTERNAL / EXTERNAL FORCE)**
Ex. Joy	Spending time in beautiful weather outside

Pay close attention the next time some of your negative triggers pop up. Can you replace that emotion by using a positive trigger? If one of your good friends made you laugh yesterday, text them when you need a smile. If being outside in nature brought you joy, take a five minute walk to cool down.

Our minds are incredibly powerful when we use them properly. There is nothing we can't achieve when we believe we can do it and when we have the mental stamina to do the work. When you think your goals are impossible or that being happier is too hard, think back to the 40% rule from the beginning of the chapter, which said that when we feel like we've hit our limit, we're really only 40% there. Can you reframe your mindset and push further? Can you take one more step in the right direction? Can you convince yourself that you are able?

Good.

Because as we move into the Emotional Pillar, all of this mental work will play a role in helping you process your own emotions and become more aware of what others (and you) are truly feeling. The Emotional Pillar is where we'll go deep in talking about your relationships and the role they play in your happiness. But before we can go there, we need to be at peace with ourselves. And that begins in our minds with the understanding that what we think and do aligns with our values.

You're strong, you have all the tools you need, and you're ready. Let's keep going.

CHAPTER 5

THE EMOTIONAL PILLAR

"Let us always meet each other with a smile,
for the smile is the beginning of love."

–MOTHER TERESA

ONE OF THE BEST THINGS about getting married is that all of the important people in your life come together in one room. Worlds collide. Your high school friends finally get to meet your work friends. Your family finally gets to meet your college buddies. And your wife's friends and family meet yours. It's a beautiful time to acknowledge all the many relationships that will end up playing a role in your marriage.

For our wedding, we invited about 200 friends and family members to celebrate with us in Newport, Rhode Island. We decided on a destination wedding since our guests were spread across the country, and we felt extremely blessed to have people travel hundreds of miles to celebrate with us. We exchanged our vows right next to the beach on a bright, sunny day, surrounded by people we love. It was everything we hoped for and more.

As we bopped from table to table at the reception, I loved hearing about the new connections our guests were making. Friends who didn't know each other but were seated at the same table were raising their glasses to toast. My brothers were dancing with Joslyn's family.

And from a large number of our guests, we heard, "Your family and friends are so nice."

One of our friends who especially left an impression was Jeff.

Jeff used to play football in the NFL and is regularly on ESPN. So it made sense that a lot of people would recognize him. It didn't matter who I was talking to—young, old, male, female, sports fan, or sports oblivious—everyone had something nice to say about him.

It's *classic* Jeff, getting along with everyone he meets.

When Joslyn worked at ESPN with Jeff, she had a feeling we'd hit it off as friends. After introducing us, she was right. Right off the bat, we talked about our families and our faith. He was interested in learning about my life and offered great perspective on some of the things I was thinking about.

Truth be told, I was pretty amazed by how many questions he asked about me, when I easily could have listened to him talk about his own life for hours. In the years since, he's become a great friend and a mentor in a lot of ways.

But when I think back to Jeff at our wedding, I still admire how easily he could find connection with everyone he met. His emotional intelligence is extremely strong.

And that's the truth. When I sat down to write this chapter, I knew I wanted to talk about the importance of emotional intelligence in our journey toward happiness. And stories about Jeff kept coming to mind.

From interactions with my buddies at the wedding to hanging out at the office with my colleagues and getting to know my friends at dinners or other outings. Everywhere Jeff goes, he makes immediate connections.

Normally, when we hear the phrase "emotional intelligence," it's in the context of business. There are countless articles out there with headlines like, "3 Crucial Ways Emotional Intelligence Will Get You That Promotion" or "These 5 CEOs Say Emotional Intelligence Is the Most Important Trait when Hiring."

The term "emotional intelligence" technically refers to both self-awareness and control over your own emotions, as well as understanding the emotions of other people. For the sake of this book, when we talk about emotional intelligence, we're talking more about the latter part of the definition—understanding the emotions of other people. I prefer to refer to controlling our own emotions as "emotional strength."

So while both emotional intelligence can certainly help you get ahead in your professional life, it's crucial in your personal life. That's because no relationship is completely one-sided. You can't lean on friends and family for support and then turn a blind eye when they need it. You can't expect them to cheer you on in times of triumph, only to ignore them when their time in the spotlight comes. In order to have healthy, deep relationships, it's important that you can recognize what others are feeling and respond accordingly.

To do so also requires that you have a good handle on your own emotions. This is where we'll build on what we learned in the Mental Pillar. With more control over your thoughts, you'll be able to pull yourself out of negative emotions more quickly and be a positive force for others. Remember: Your negative mood has negative side effects for others, too. Your energy is contagious. Emotional strength on its own will play a large role in maintaining healthy, positive relationships, and it will also help you on your way to building emotional intelligence (and eventually your happiness).

So how are these things really connected, you may ask. Why the focus on relationships in the Emotional Pillar? If we can control our emotions, we're done right? We choose happiness. We're good to go. We can end the book, right?

We're getting darn close! But keep in mind that the goal isn't fleeting happiness. It's to make happiness a habit and to seek lasting fulfillment. We're playing a long game here, friends. And there's proof that relationships are key to this long-term happiness.

A Harvard study followed 700+ participants over the course of 75 years and found this: **"Good relationships keep us happier and healthier. Period."**[13]

Overwhelmingly, the research showed that the participants' happiness was linked to their relationships. Those who had deep, meaningful relationships experienced a better quality of life. And it wasn't enough just to know a large number of people. The real key to "good" relationships lied in emotional connection with others.

If that's not proof enough that relationships should be a priority, I'm not sure what is. So in this chapter, we're going to start by looking inward (building emotional strength) and then spend time looking outward (growing our emotional intelligence). Together, you will see the enormous impact they can have on your relationships and, as a result, your happiness.

LOOKING INWARD: BUILDING EMOTIONAL STRENGTH

Have you ever asked someone how they are, only to have them respond by saying, "If I were any better, I'd be twins"?

If you're in the right mood for that kind of positivity, you may laugh. Or you may roll your eyes at the overly cheerful sentiment. *Who could possibly be* that *happy?*

I have to admit something here: I love saying that to people.

---

13 https://medium.com/the-mission/want-a-happier-more-fulfilling-life-75-year-harvard-study-says-focus-on-this-1-thing-714e22c99ffc

I truly enjoy catching people off guard when they ask how I am in the morning. Remember the boring conversation we talked about last chapter? The one that followed this pattern:

PERSON 1: Hi, how are you?

PERSON 2: Good. Busy, but good. You?

PERSON 1: Same here.

Imagine what would happen if Person 2 responded by saying, "Man, I am doing *excellent!*"

You may think, *Excellent, huh? What's so excellent about a normal morning?*

And that is exactly why I do it. When I can throw someone off with my response (and truly believe and feel it), it gets them thinking about the way this conversation normally goes. They may not totally understand why I'm so upbeat at that moment, but hopefully they also start to question if they're really just "fine" or "good" or "okay." Maybe—just maybe—I can get them to feel a little bit better about their own morning and change their state of mind. Maybe they'll think about what they're grateful for that day. It's a small gesture, but you never know how it may impact someone else.

And as you can imagine, it helps to affirm that I really will have an excellent day. I like to think of it as a testament to my own emotional strength. When I vocalize that I'm doing fantastic, I'm not going to let anything bring me down that day.

Now, emotional strength can mean different things to many people. But one of the biggest misconceptions is that emotionally strong people have to go through intense trauma in order to build up that strength. Have you ever listened to a motivational speaker give a speech? Many of those speeches begin with a "rock bottom" story, an anecdote about a time in their life when they knew things couldn't get any worse. When they realized that they would need to dig their way out of whatever circumstances were causing their unhappiness.

When I think of emotional strength, there are certainly some people who have experienced far worse than I have who come to mind. But I truly believe that emotional strength is something each and every one of us can build, no matter what life throws our way.

You see, when I think about emotional strength, I think about experiencing everything that life has to offer. There will be hard times, sure. Negative emotions will come up from time to time. But while we can acknowledge the painful times, emotional strength means working through them and experiencing the good *fully*. We spend far too much time in a state of what I like to call "okayishness."

Okayishness is the feeling that accompanies responses like "fine" or "good" or "okay." Is that really all you are? Or have you conditioned yourself to think that your everyday state—one in which you are not currently experiencing anything difficult or painful—is just okay?

In the future when someone asks you how you are, I want you to respond by saying, "Excellent!" And I want you to truly mean it, feel it, and believe it. You'll get there by training yourself to see the positive aspects in life and by working through the negative stuff. *That* is emotional strength.

WHAT EMOTIONAL STRENGTH IS NOT

Another common misconception about emotional strength is that it means being happy all the time. When something bad happens, emotionally strong people snap their fingers and immediately get over it. We may even look at hyper-positive people and think that they're just burying their emotions deep down. In other words, they're not really living life like the rest of us.

I want to make it super clear that I understand negative emotions are a part of life. There is no magic button to press that makes pain or heartache go away. When life throws things our way, we can't snap our fingers or imagine a half-full glass of water and instantly feel better.

Instead, when you feel pain or negativity, feel it. Acknowledge it. But don't stay there.

Let's think back to the river metaphor one more time here. We've got our paddles—mental strength and mental curiosity—to help us navigate the rocks and boulders in the river. Emotional strength is the muscle power you need to move the paddles. Without those paddles, there'd be nothing more you could do. You'd just sail down the river, frantically splashing your hands in the water and bumping into anything in your path. But with those paddles in hand, along with the muscle to push and pull them, you are able to steer yourself where you want to go.

When the rapids pick up, you may have to do a little more work. If there's a huge rock in your path, you may need to put all of your strength into getting around it. Those muscles may get fatigued from time to time. You may feel more bumps and turbulence. You may even have to get out of the boat and carry it.

Emotional strength is not just about taking a smooth sail down the river, worry free. And it's not usually about having a near-death experience where you have to fight off a school of piranhas either. It's about simply doing what you can to enjoy the boat trip.

Because, in this metaphor, you only get one trip on a boat. Let's make it count.

BUILDING EMOTIONAL STRENGTH

The key to building emotional strength is to use everyday experiences to help prepare you for harder things down the road. We are presented with countless opportunities everyday to take more control over our emotions.

So I'm going to share five tools here that will help you to turn negative emotions into positive or, at the very least, neutral ones. Here's what we'll talk about:

- How to find the good in things in life
- Why you should face your fears
- Spending time around optimistic people
- Talking to yourself
- How to use physical activity and breathing to create calm

If you haven't already started daily challenges from the Emotional section in the back of the book, go ahead and do so now. You'll find some challenges that relate to each of these tools, and I encourage you to try them out as we go.

Let's start with one we hear about most often—finding a silver lining.

FIND THE GOOD

It's so easy, right? Just look on the bright side. Find the good.

Normally when we talk about silver linings or looking for the good in a situation, we're saying it in consolatory terms. We're sorry that a bad thing happened, but at least there's this tiny, little piece of good that came from it.

A silver lining can make us feel slightly better but usually not much. And the reason it doesn't have a huge impact is because we're not in the practice of looking for it regularly. It's hard to find a silver lining when we're really upset.

But when we practice gratitude on a regular basis, it's not so hard. We're able to put negative emotions into a larger context. We're able weigh the bad versus the good more easily.

There is a quote I love by Henri Matisse that reads, "There are always flowers for those who want to see them." If we want to see the positive aspects in our lives, we can always view them. But if we're only bringing them to mind in the face of something negative, they lose some power. The best way to fully experience the good in your life, to bask in what you have, is to regularly practice gratitude.

This may mean thinking about three things you're grateful for each morning. It could mean putting away your cell phone at dinner and enjoying your family fully. It could mean taking a small moment of silence to yourself at an event like a birthday party or wedding to acknowledge your happiness in that instant.

There may be times when you'll want to explain away negative emotions by pointing to outside circumstances. Raise your hand if you're pretty grumpy in the morning before your first cup of coffee or if you have ever told someone that you let your temper "get the better of you." These kinds of everyday excuses only end up validating your negative emotions. They make it sound like your mood is completely out of your hands, when in fact you control both your temper and your coffee consumption.

Don't wait for something negative to happen in your life to look for a silver lining, and don't underestimate the power you have over those negative occasions. Practice recognizing what you are grateful for every day, and you will be able to roll with the small punches more easily. And when the big ones come, you'll be able to start the healing process more quickly.

FACE YOUR FEARS

Fear is a powerful emotion, and it's one that has its benefits. The fight-or-flight impulse is important for our survival instincts, and it helps us make "gut instinct" decisions.

All too often, though, fear gets in the way of things we want to accomplish. We fear failure, so we never start. We fear embarrassment, so we don't put our ideas out there. We fear disappointing people we care about, so we maintain the status quo. We fear being judged, so we don't truly follow our passions.

Learning how to face these kinds of fears head-on is important to achieving your goals. Take some time to think about your idea of happiness. Is there anything about it that scares you or makes you nervous? Is there a reason you haven't already gone after it?

Make it a goal to face that fear head-on, and give yourself a time frame. If you want to start a business but fear of failure is keeping you from quitting your day job, give yourself a deadline for getting it done. Put whatever safety nets in place you can, like putting more money into savings, and tell someone about your plan to keep you accountable. Don't allow fear to compel you to keep putting off your dreams. Instead, focus on courage and face your fears head-on.

If that sounds terrifying, start small. Start by facing a smaller fear to create some momentum. Trust me, once you've gotten past your fear of dogs or flying or heights, you'll feel motivated to keep tackling bigger fears, like public speaking.

By engaging with the things you fear, you will not only have a better understanding of your emotional state but you'll also be removing a potential roadblock from experiencing joy fully. By overcoming your fear of dogs, you may find companionship. You may experience a culture you'd only dreamed of by getting past your fear of flying. You might even meet the love of your life at the top of the Empire State Building once you face your fear of heights. Who knows!

The point is that by facing your fears, you are removing a potential excuse to not go after the life you want and you are taking control of one of the biggest negative emotions we face.

SPEND TIME AROUND OPTIMISTIC PEOPLE

I've said it before, and I'll say it again. The people you spend time with will have a tremendous impact on you. If you want to experience the joys of life more fully, it's imperative that you spend more time around positive, uplifting people.

I know that ending relationships and friendships may sound a little selfish or harsh, but your life is too short to spend time with people that don't lift you up—and that you aren't able to lift up in return.

A common response I've heard from people when I'm trying to lift their moods is that they're just being "real." In other words, they think that they're living in the real world by acknowledging its real problems, while optimistic people must be shoving down their feelings or ignoring reality altogether. Well, my response to that is who can say what is "real" when it comes to emotions? If two people get into fender benders one morning, is the person who stews over it all day somehow experiencing more of the real world than the person who calls insurance, deals with the problem, and moves on? Is either person's experience more "real"? It's likely you'll encounter some pushback from pessimists like this along the way, but pay that negativity no attention.

Find people instead who make you smile, who encourage you to be your best, who challenge you to chase your dreams, who can always find the good in others, and who genuinely love life. I promise you will leave all of those interactions feeling better than before. You will feel full instead of drained. And you'll be able to share that positive energy with other people in your life.

Remember, you can meet new people all over the place. Ask your friends to introduce you to their other friends. Join a league or a meet-up group. Try out a church. Join a professional organization. In other words, put yourself out there and remain open to new relationships. When you find someone who is optimistic and uplifting, who you feel a connection with, make that relationship a priority.

TALK TO YOURSELF

You read that right. I'd like us to practice talking to ourselves. The good news? We already do it all the time. In our minds.

According to a History Channel documentary about the human brain, the average person says 300–1,000 words to themselves each minute.[14] Our brains are talkative! And within all that chatter, there's tremendous opportunity.

Is the majority of what we're saying positive or negative? Are we doubting ourselves all the time, or are we cheering ourselves on?

The documentary covers our good friends, the Navy SEALs, and shows the impact that positive self-talk can have on training pass rates. Those who can positively talk themselves through each step, as opposed to thinking that they may fail or don't have what it takes, are more likely to make it through.

This comes in handy particularly in underwater exercises where trainers simulate attacks by disabling the trainees' scuba equipment. Pretty terrifying, right? Well, the SEALs that tell themselves to remember their training and to focus on the next step in fixing the situation experience much greater success in the exercise than those that focus on their fear of drowning.

Self-talk is incredibly important in getting through situations that cause you fear, but it's also a useful habit to get into to help you deal with a range of negative emotions. Take note of when your mind veers to negative self-talk. Snap a rubber band on your wrist or make a tally on a piece of paper, and actively try to shift your mind to encouraging self-talk.

State your goals out loud. Pump yourself up in front of a mirror. Then talk to your family or friends. Self-talk can be a game changer. While it may seem silly at first, remember it's only because you haven't made

---

14   https://www.amazon.com/Brain-DVD-Richard-Vagg/dp/B001J863EO

this a habit. But getting where you want to be means doing something different.

GET MOVING

We talked in the Physical Pillar about the benefit of physical fitness on our emotions, but it bears repeating here. Doing something physical, even simply walking for a few minutes, can instantly boost your mood.

The link between physical activity and mood is strong. So when you feel negative emotions bubbling up inside of you, make a point to step away and go for a quick walk. This is almost always a good idea before you shoot off an angry text or email.

And getting in the habit of regular exercise will also help you to head off negative emotions to start with. Activity does not need to be done in reaction to negative emotions. Rather, it should be part of your everyday life.

Another aspect of this link between our emotions and our bodies that we haven't talked about yet is the power of breathing. In the first yoga class I went to, I remember having difficulty taking such deep breaths. We'd breathe in for several seconds, hold it, and breathe out slowly. It felt wonderful and calming, but it did make me realize how infrequently I took such deep breaths. I was way out of practice.

After that, I got in the habit of practicing four-square breathing, also known as box breathing. Four-square breathing is often a big part of meditation practices and has been shown to calm stress. All you do is breathe in for four seconds, hold for four seconds, breathe out for four seconds, hold for four seconds.

If you're not in a position to leave what you're doing and take a walk, four-square breathing can be an equally powerful alternative. After all, no matter what you're doing, you need to breathe at the same time. So whether you're standing in line for something, sitting at your desk, or watching TV, practice this kind of breathing. And when something stressful comes along, go back to it.

Through regular physical activity and practicing four-square breathing, you'll be setting yourself up to have a positive outlook day after day, and you'll also have some tools in your back pocket for dealing with more stressful or painful situations as they come.

None of the tools I've shared here need a negative event to trigger them. They are things you can practice every single day if you want to. At first, they'll help you get over small annoyances here and there, like running late for work or the trash bag breaking on you. But over time, they'll help you through harder times. They'll help you muscle your way around some pretty big boulders.

Again, when those negative emotions come up, acknowledge them. Feel them. But don't stay there. Take the time you need to process and maybe even grieve. When you're ready to move forward, these same tools will be there for you to help you on your way. But before something truly negative happens, you'll feel a deeper connection with the positive aspects of your life every day. You will feel that happiness and positivity *fully*.

The other half of the Emotional Pillar is about looking outward to the people you'll encounter in your life. How can you build connection with them? How can that connection support your happiness? That's where emotional intelligence comes into play.

LOOKING OUTWARD: CULTIVATING EMOTIONAL INTELLIGENCE

It's not always easy to listen to someone complain or to see someone cycle through the same negative emotions time after time. But, while some people are chronic complainers, most people who come to you really just need someone to lean on. One of the best skills you can learn is to put yourself in their shoes and to think about what they need from you in that particular instance.

Developing a sense of emotional intelligence, and the empathy that entails, ultimately plays into everything you do. When you meet someone at a party, are you paying attention to their body language or what they're saying? Or are you worried about what you'll say next?

Do you write off high-touch clients at work as crazy? Or do you see where they're coming from most of the time?

Do you make friends easily? Or does it feel like a struggle?

There are many reasons why developing emotional intelligence is important, and one of the most basic is that it helps guide you through social interactions. And as we've talked about before, there's just no getting around interacting with people. You *have* to do it. So even if you consider yourself an introvert and dislike social situations, there are many simple ways to improve and make socializing less painful.

Another important benefit of emotional intelligence is that it helps to draw the right people to you. If your network is your net worth, how can you expand or improve that network? Meeting new people and developing a close enough relationship with them so that you may lean on them for advice or mentorship can be tough. But emotional intelligence makes it easier.

And once you're surrounded by the people you want, emotional intelligence also allows you to go deeper in your relationships with them. By understanding their feelings and drives, you are able to be there for them in a meaningful way when they need it. By doing so, you'll validate their feelings, and you'll share a deeper friendship or connection.

And last but not least, emotional intelligence matters in a business setting. At the beginning of the chapter, I mentioned that we almost always hear the term thrown around in business articles or in terms of what emotionally intelligent employees stand to gain. And it's absolutely true. Emotionally intelligent employees collaborate better with others, respond to feedback better, and listen to their teammates. As a result, they're more likely to make good decisions at work and may even see greater career growth over time.

It all sounds great, right? The more we're able to relate to other people, the the more we start to meet some of our goals. And the more we really start to engage with life. But I recognize that working and interacting with other people isn't always easy. Sometimes the act of thinking about another person's feelings—particularly someone that's difficult to get along with—can be downright hard.

Here's how to do it.

HOW TO IMPROVE

One question I get often is, "Do I really need to put myself in everyone's shoes? Aren't some people unkind and undeserving of my empathy?"

To that, I respond, yes. Yes, it's important that you practice empathy with everyone you come into contact with. The person at work who always complains. The waiter who gives you terrible service. The driver who flips you the bird. The homeless person on the corner. The friend who voted for the other political party.

It can be so easy to typecast the people we come into contact with and write them off as whatever stereotype comes to mind. But if we want to build deeper connections with the people around us, it starts by breaking down assumptions like this that can get in the way. If we write someone off who's been complaining a lot as a Debbie Downer, we may not see that they're going through a hard time or the real potential for friendship there.

Have you ever said or done something that you regretted? Something you looked back on and thought, *Man, that's not me.*

Stephen M.R. Covey said, "We judge ourselves by our intentions and others by their behaviour." And that's so true. We cut ourselves breaks for bad behavior because we know that our intentions were good. But when it comes to other people, we're often not so forgiving.

So the first step to developing emotional intelligence that we'll talk about is trying to break that habit, to stop judging people only by their actions and to consider their possible intentions.

THINK ABOUT INTENTIONS

I'm a pretty tidy person for the most part. When I lived with roommates in college, I was often the one cleaning up the common areas. It was a relief to move in with Joslyn after we got married because we both shared high standards for cleanliness.

But occasionally Joslyn would leave some clothes on the floor or the dresser, like a normal human being. There were times when I thought, *She knows this bugs me. Why would she do this?*

A little melodramatic, right? But we're all often quick to assume that when someone we care about does something we don't like, it's because they're out to annoy us. Think about your pet peeves for a second. When someone you care about does one of them, doesn't it feel like a personal affront?

But, as was the case with the clothes on the floor, it often has very little to do with us. When I stopped to think about it, I knew that Joslyn wasn't thinking, *Perfect. I'll put these clothes here and it will drive Aaron crazy. My evil genius plan to make him miserable starts now.*

She was thinking, *I have a big day at work and need to get there early. I'll tackle this later this evening.*

Again, totally normal!

The truth is that stopping to consider a person's real intentions only requires one thing: stopping. It requires pulling yourself out of your normal thought patterns and giving a few more seconds to the situation at hand.

In those seconds, ask yourself:

‣ How likely is it that this action has anything to do with me?

‣ Are there circumstances in their life that I know about that may drive this action?

‣ What are some possible intentions behind the action?

There may be some situations where a person really is out to annoy you or hurt you. When someone repeatedly shows you who they are, believe them. But the vast majority of people are not out to hurt anyone else, so try to cut them some slack the first time they do something hurtful. Chances are they're just reacting to the world around them in a way that has become habit or in a way that has been modeled for them by others.

This doesn't mean that I'm suggesting you become a pushover, that you let the people around you behave however they want and say nothing. All I'm suggesting is to stop and think about the other person's intentions before reacting, especially on the first offense. When you are able to react from a place of understanding or empathy, it's likely you'll have a better conversation.

Imagine that I had reacted in anger to Joslyn or passive aggressively moved those clothes to another spot. I'd be telling her that my happiness is more important than her big day at work. But by taking a step back to think about her intentions, I was able to put everything into context. Of course laundry isn't more important. So rather than get mad or annoyed, I decided to do something nice for her. I put them away where they belonged so that she wouldn't need to worry about it later. So that we could talk about her big day instead. No big deal.

These kinds of selfless acts can bring real joy. It's a little like exercising—you may not want to do it at first, but you almost never regret it after. Doing something selfless and caring for someone else is something you just won't regret doing, especially if you keep in mind that selflessness means not expecting anything in return.

So whether you're married to someone or just met them, considering the possible intentions driving their actions will help you to respond from a place of kindness and understanding. You may never actually find out their real intentions, but there is enormous benefit to be gained by assuming those intentions are positive.

PAY ATTENTION TO BODY LANGUAGE

A person's body language can tell you a lot about how they're feeling. If their arms are crossed or their shoulders are slumped, that person may not be in the best mood. If they're smiling with relaxed arms, chances are they're feeling good.

Just as we have to pay attention to how we come off to others, it's important that we pay attention to how others present themselves to us, especially the people we know well. I can tell instantly when one of my siblings is upset. They don't have to say a word, and I know that I need to shift gears and listen to their concerns.

Do you know your friends' or family's silent cues? Can you pick up on their feelings without them telling you? I'm sure that, for some people, you absolutely can. If not, just start paying more attention to it. When someone is feeling down, pay attention to how they sit, how they walk, the facial expressions they make, and where their eyes travel. Do the same when that person is feeling great. We may not know all the cues for these emotions or even understand why we know them, but if we pay closer attention, we can find out.

Start to notice these kinds of behaviors with the people closest to you, and you'll be able to pick up on patterns that translate to other people outside your network. When you meet someone at a party, are they crossing their arms and legs, physically closing themselves off? Or is their body language loose and open? Do they need someone to help make them comfortable in that setting? Or are they looking for someone to joke around with?

When you recognize the silent cues that people around you are giving, you can adjust your own behavior accordingly. This doesn't necessarily mean turning into a yes-man and doing everything you can to make someone like you. It just means communicating with people in a way that will resonate with them. By doing so, you're leaving the door open for deeper connection.

If you're talking to a person that's showing signs of being uncomfortable at the party, and all you do is crack jokes and introduce them to other people, you may be contributing to their discomfort. Instead, you may ask them some questions about what they're interested in, move the conversation to a calmer area of the party, or introduce them to someone you genuinely think they'd hit it off with.

By paying attention to the body language of other people, you'll be better equipped to navigate social settings and to take greater control of those interactions. If you're a naturally shy person, body language can give you a leg up in talking with others, making it less intimidating. And the biggest payoff of all—you'll be able to recognize when other people need your help before they have to ask for it.

PRACTICE EMPATHY

Practice. Practice. Practice. That's what it all comes down to. To get better at anything, practice is required. Emotional intelligence is no different. Over time, you'll get better at recognizing other people's possible intentions and reading their body language. Just by bringing awareness to those things, you will be better able to recognize them.

Once you've done that and you've recognized that someone may need to lean on you, the next step is to be there for them, and that is easier said than done.

What does it mean to really be there for another person?

Does it mean simply listening while they talk? Does it mean sending them flowers or chocolates? Does it mean praying for them? Or all of the above?

Being there for another person means something different to each person. All too often, we come up with a definition of support that's based on what we would like for ourselves. When *I'm* upset, I appreciate when someone says that they'll pray over it. So my impulse may be to tell other people that I'll pray for them too when they need it.

But to a nonreligious person, that means very little. I'm not being there for them in the way that *they* need. In a way that will provide comfort to that specific person. When I'm upset, I like for someone to listen to me and then point out the positive side for me. But I know that if I do that for others, sometimes too much positivity can rub people the wrong way.

Treating other people the way we want to be treated is the golden rule for a reason. In 99% of cases, it serves us well. But sometimes, it's important to treat other people the way *they* want to be treated. And so when we practice empathy, we have to keep this in mind.

So how do we do that, then? How do we know the right way to respond?

Imagine that, when someone needs you, you hold out your hand to them. You could hold out a closed fist or a flat palm. But what you want to hold out is a cupped hand, open and available to cradle someone's emotions. In that hand, you want to hold those emotions. Feel them. Validate them.

The hand symbolizes approaching another person's emotions without judgment or expectation. It's about feeling those emotions alongside them. It's about letting the other person know that you hear them, you understand them, and you support them.

You do not need to fix someone's problems right away. You don't need to rush to offer your prayers or send them a card. The best thing to do is to approach them with openness and to cradle those feelings for them. A shared emotional experience is a much more powerful antidote than a sympathy card.

Remember that just as you will move on from negative emotions in your own time, so too will the other people in your life. Keep in mind that they may need to sit in those emotions for longer than you do. They may need more support from others than you do. Understand that their emotional journey will look different than yours and offer your help in ways that you think will matter to *them*.

When you experience negative emotions, you want to feel them. Acknowledge them. But don't stay there.

Be a positive force to help others move forward, too.

EMOTIONAL STRENGTH + INTELLIGENCE = RELATIONSHIP GOLD

When I look back at our wedding, I still laugh at my buddy Jeff and his ability to make friends with everyone he met. But I also look back on it as a moment of pride in myself and Joslyn. To look around a room and see everyone that we care about, everyone that we chose to be a part of our lives, was a pretty special moment.

I am so grateful for the relationships I've formed over the years. They are one of the biggest sources of happiness in my life, and as a result, some of the things I value most in life are family and friendship.

In the Mental Pillar, I asked if you thought you'd be able to name your top values in life if I were to put you on the spot. We're working toward being able to answer that question, but there's one thing I'd like to plant in your mind now as we continue to think about it. Most people that I know place other people somewhere in their top values, whether it's family or friends or simply helping other people through volunteer work or philanthropy.

As the Harvard study pointed out, relationships are often the most important factor in a happy life. But by understanding which relationships in particular bring us the most joy, we're able to intentionally cultivate them. In other words, we're connecting to our "why" once again. If we value family, that should come through in everything we do. We should make time for them and nurture those relationships.

If we value helping people, we should constantly strive to understand their needs and emotions. We should make volunteering a priority and schedule time for it every week.

But above all, if we're to interact deeply with other people, we need to understand that doing so is an emotional experience. We need to be aware of our own emotions and take control of them instead of letting them control us.

We need to judge others not always by their actions but by their intentions. We need to pay attention to the silent cues they give us about what they're looking for. And most of all, we need to share in their emotions and allow them to share in ours.

By doing so, we'll take part in one of the greatest joys available to us: human connection.

In the next Pillar, we'll be discussing spirituality, another amazing gift available to us. Just as with this chapter, I encourage you to go into it with an open mind. Allow yourself to play and experiment and find what works for you.

Ready to dive in?

CHAPTER 6

THE SPIRITUAL PILLAR

"As iron sharpens iron, so one person sharpens another"

—PROVERBS 27:17

GROWING UP, THERE WASN'T a Sunday that my family missed church. The six of us would have some breakfast together, get dressed in our church clothes, and pile in our van. We always sat in the same section of pews and shook hands with fellow church goers and the families we had become friends with.

With four kids in soccer and an endless stream of weekend tournaments, it wasn't always an easy task to get us all to church. And there were plenty of instances where we'd have to change out of church clothes and into uniforms in the van on the way to a game.

It wasn't exactly convenient, but it was clear to all of us how much joy my mother got from us going to mass together every week and from teaching the Word to her children.

My mom has always been the quiet spiritual leader of our house. And while we did enjoy our Sunday ritual too, it was for Mom that we made no exceptions about missing mass. And when we would walk up to the altar for Holy Communion, she happily led the pack of us kids.

When you're a child, you might go through the motions of church for a while before you really understand what's going on. It took me a while to realize that other dads didn't always hang back at Communion time. In the Catholic faith, only Catholics receive the Eucharist. My dad was born in Libya and was raised in a different faith. So for as long as I could remember, we'd file out of the pew and leave our dad quietly sitting in prayer. That was just how it was for us, and we never thought anything of it.

Week after week, there he was, joining us in church despite not being a full-fledged member of it. He did it because he knew how important it was to raise his children following the Lord, because he saw how much my mom loved (and still loves) her faith, and because he saw how happy it made her to share that faith with her family, whether or not they participated fully.

I was never aware of any talks of conversion while growing up, but there was plenty of talk of faith. If we had questions after church, my mom was always available to talk and to tell us her thoughts. She encouraged us to pray but was never demanding. To this day, she continues to be a steady, quiet force, an example of someone deeply connected to her faith.

Despite this upbringing of regular churchgoing, I fell away from faith in college. I tried out the local mass a few times, but something felt off. I didn't feel a connection to church anymore. I questioned what to believe. I still prayed occasionally and felt a spiritual connection to something bigger, but I didn't know exactly what.

I guess that's pretty normal for a college kid. There are other things to think about and more fun things to do on a Sunday than head to church. I was having the time of my life; why would I want to think of bigger, more existential things?

Oddly enough, I never felt like I should lie to my mom about this period of my life. When she'd call and ask what I was up to that weekend, I never slipped in that I was going to church just to make her feel better. In fact, I was honest with her about the disconnect I felt, and we had several conversations about it.

She'd listen. She'd ask questions. She'd answer the questions I had. And she'd tell me she loved me.

A few years later, something remarkable happened. I felt the urge to go to church again. My professional life was going well, and I had made some great friendships. By all accounts, I seemed happy, but I felt a gap. I felt like there had to be something more.

I saw a sign for a Christian church service one day and decided to stop in. In a lot of ways, it was very different than what I was used to. Instead of a choir, there was a band. Instead of a robed priest, there was a pastor. It's hard to articulate what I felt that day, but suffice it to say that something felt *right*.

Around the same time, my dad made the decision to convert to Catholicism. After 25 years of accompanying my mom to church, he made a decision to join the faith fully—to devote his life to God and follow His lead. No matter what was going on in my own spiritual path, I was proud of him and admired him at the same time.

And throughout all of this, my mom listened. She asked questions. She encouraged that we explore our faith. And she loved us.

I will always appreciate my mom for these moments. She loves her faith. She radiates joy when she talks about it. And what she wanted most for us was that we feel the same. That we don't go to church to go through the motions or to please someone else, but that we go because we also love our faith. I didn't realize it at the time, but every action she took planted seeds for a strong spiritual life that would take a while to grow and bloom fully.

As we talk about this chapter, I'll share a little more about my journey to faith. But I'd like to start off by taking a page from my mom's book and making it clear that I'm not here to dictate your path for you. There are countless benefits to living a spiritual life—longer lifespans, a sense of community, ethical guidance, and so on—that I encourage you to take part in. And there are many ways to do just that.

So, while my own Christian faith is incredibly important to me and guides me in everything I do, I'm not here to to tell you what to do. But I'll ask questions. I'll encourage you. And I'll support you.

You may also be wondering at this point how spirituality fits into the larger framework of this book. If you think back again to high school psych class, Maslow's hierarchy of needs tells us that we need to feel things like belonging and self-esteem before we are able to achieve self-actualization, the highest level of the pyramid. In other words, in order to make sense of the meaning and value of life, it's important to understand yourself as best you can first. Doing so is also pivotal to making sure that you aren't pushed into someone else's idea of spirituality.

Now that we've done the work of getting to know ourselves, we're ready to take on this chapter. Spirituality isn't the easiest thing for many people to talk about, so things may not always feel comfortable as you work through it. But I encourage you to go in with an open mind, allow yourself to be vulnerable, and try things out. Allow yourself to experiment and discover what makes sense for you.

But before we get into all that, let's define faith, shall we?

WHAT IS FAITH?

When we think about faith, there are a number of things that come to mind. Most often, we think of the word only in combination with a modern religion, like Christianity, Judaism, Hinduism, or Islam. In that sense, the definition of faith changes and morphs depending on the lens of the religion we view it through. We start to tack on additional meanings to the word. We think that one person's faith must be vastly different from another's.

But I'm not going to overcomplicate things, here.

Faith, put simply, is believing in something that you cannot see.

Faith is understanding what you can and *cannot* control. It's about trusting some higher force. It's about acknowledging that there is something more.

One of the most difficult aspects of faith is that it often isn't very logical, especially to new believers. You can't reason your way into believing something you can't see. I mentioned earlier that I went through a period of feeling disconnected from my own faith. One of the most frustrating aspects of that time was that I struggled to vocalize *why* I felt disconnected. I couldn't quite put my finger on it. And when I found my current church, I couldn't quite put my finger on why it felt right—why that sense of connection returned.

You can choose to express your faith through the religion you follow or by simply connecting to the idea that there is a higher power at play. But I will say that there are some benefits to joining a spiritual community that we'll talk about shortly. So if it doesn't sound appealing off the bat, don't write it off quite yet.

And no matter how difficult faith can be to talk about, it's a conversation worth having because, by having it, we're able to grow in our faith, test our ideas, and build an even deeper connection with those around us.

WHY IS TALKING ABOUT FAITH SO DIFFICULT?

The first time I went to my current church, all of my impulses were telling me not to go in. I was nervous what I'd find inside. Truth be told, I wasn't even sure what I was hoping I'd find in there. But I opened the door, walked in, and found a spot to myself in one of the back pews. I figured no one in the back would notice me or try to make conversation.

But when the service was over, the people sitting around me introduced themselves and told me about a breakfast happening in the cafeteria. They'd have coffee and bagels, and it was a chance for the congregation to get to know each other and connect each week. I very easily could have told them that I needed to be somewhere and slip out (and I thought about doing just that). But since I enjoyed the service even more than I expected and felt truly filled with up with God's Word that day, I decided to give it a shot. Together, we walked to the breakfast, and they introduced me around to people. I was overwhelmed by the kindness I was met with in return.

When a group of new acquaintances invited me to lunch the following week, I only hesitated a bit before saying yes. Soon after, I happily joined a small group, or Bible study, once a week, and when they asked for volunteers to lead us in prayer, I raised my hand. I didn't have a lot of practice praying out loud on behalf of a group, or actually any experience at all, but I decided to just throw myself into it.

Quite frankly, I was nervous. I was brand new to the whole Bible study thing and had no idea what to say. But I reminded myself that every pro was once an amateur and decided to simply give it a go.

Over time, the part of me that was nervous or hesitant started to fall by the wayside. But it took time. At almost every step of the way, my impulses were telling me to run away. And yet, after every interaction, I found a deeper sense of comfort and calm. I found a mentor who I'm able to dig deeper with on topics I may not fully understand and who has been instrumental in my spiritual growth. I developed a stronger connection to Christ. I felt like I was a little bit closer to discovering what had been missing in my life.

Why, then, had I been so hesitant at first?

The truth is that I was uncomfortable with the idea of faith. I felt vulnerable when people I barely knew asked intimate, existential questions. I felt insecure when I didn't know certain Bible verses by heart. I was nervous that people were only being nice to me to try to get me to join *their* faith, *their* community and that these potential friendships could just disappear if I didn't.

What I experienced were pretty common emotions when it comes to faith. Discomfort. Vulnerability. Insecurity. Nervousness. Doubt. But there are so many positives on the other side, when you move past those emotions—the Fruits of the Spirit, so to speak.

VULNERABILITY REQUIRED

On the day I saw the sign for the church service and decided to give it a try, I was walking my dog Zane through town. We took walks every day and must have passed the church more times than I could count.

That morning, I was questioning my own happiness. I had been living according to my motto of being better than I was yesterday for a few years already, and I knew that my overall goal for that lifestyle was to feel true and lasting peace of mind. I wanted to go to sleep at night knowing I had done what I could to live life fully, be a part of this world, and make an impact.

I was busy, no doubt. From morning to night, I kept striving for improvement. I met a buddy at the gym at 5:30 a.m. every day, worked long hours, went to happy hours or sports leagues in the evenings, and tried to read books before bed. Day in and day out, I kept a fast pace and saw it pay off, particularly at work.

And yet, I didn't always feel a sense of calm. My mind wasn't really at peace.

On that walk, I felt tired. I felt down on myself for not being truly happy with all that I had. And I felt like a bit of a failure for not being able to sustain my active lifestyle.

It was the first moment of quiet and stillness that I could remember in months. And you know what happened? That stillness allowed some honest thoughts to creep in. I admitted to myself that all the professional success in the world wasn't going to be enough. I admitted that the friends I was spending time with weren't filling me up fully. I needed a deeper connection to myself and to the people in my life. To something more.

And then, like a sign from God, I saw the sign for the church service. Only it had been there all along. It wasn't new, and I didn't serendipitously stumble upon it after deciding to take a different walking route on a whim. No, the only difference was that I opened my eyes to it. And that started with stillness, with honesty, and with the vulnerability to admit I didn't have all the answers.

There's no getting around the fact that faith is a deeply personal topic. It was hard enough to admit to myself that I was feeling a gap. It was equally hard to start sharing my newfound faith with others.

One reason we feel discomfort when asked about our beliefs is that answering those questions requires a great deal of introspection. We need to ask ourselves some bigger questions like, what guides you? What's important to you? What are your personal ethics? How do you want to treat others? And in order to address those questions, we need to be vulnerable with ourselves and to answer with absolute honesty.

For many of us, it's a lot easier to go through our routines—go to work, meet friends, make dinner, watch TV, repeat—than it is to take time for serious reflection. I was a perfect example of that for a while. And then when we do reflect, we may need to come face-to-face with actions we've taken that fly in the face of what we believe are our personal ethics, like spending time with people who negatively influence you. Guilty again.

Allow yourself, also, to admit what you don't know, to explore without expectations, and to accept that you don't have to believe the same way others do, including those closest to you. Allow yourself to be completely vulnerable in your thoughts.

For those in the early stages of exploring faith, introspection should also be done in combination with exploration. This may mean asking questions of other people about their beliefs, reading about theology or ethics, or trying out a few churches. We'll talk about other ways to explore faith in just a bit, but for now keep in mind that, while self-reflection is a relatively solitary activity, you can also do some research to give you some things to evaluate and think about along the way.

And, when you're ready, allow that vulnerability to spread to your conversations with others. One of the biggest benefits to spirituality and faith is the opportunity for community, for the possibility of sharing your beliefs with like-minded people. But sharing your beliefs can also mean leaving yourself open to criticism or judgment.

When I went to lunch with my new buddies from church, one of them asked me what I thought of the service. How do you quickly sum up your thoughts about something so deep as heaven or hell? As your core belief system? I found myself stumbling over my thoughts. I hadn't worked through them on my own enough to share them with others at that point. And what if I said something they disagreed with?

When it comes to faith, there's no uniform consensus among all 7.5 billion of us on Earth about the right way to live or the right path to salvation. For me, I know that my absolute is Jesus Christ as Lord and Savior, but faith requires trust in what you personally believe but do not see. Every time you talk to someone about your faith, you run the risk of facing some opposing views, but that doesn't mean the conversation isn't worth having.

In fact, it's worth embracing, and by discussing your beliefs, you'll likely consider aspects of them you hadn't before. You may unlock new depths to your faith. You may feel more secure in it. So my recommendation for having these conversations is to go into them with a sense of curiosity and honesty. You don't need to mirror what the person in front of you believes, and you don't need to prove them wrong. Just let a little vulnerability in and see what you find.

THE FRUITS OF FAITH

Despite the fact that faith is a hugely vulnerable subject, I hope I didn't scare you off from it! There are some enormous benefits to getting vulnerable and engaging in a religious community. In fact, study after study has shown that religious people tend to be happier than nonreligious people.[15] And across these studies, it's not just one religion that stands out. Rather, it has more to do with the sense of community and ethical guidance that nearly all modern religions evoke.

I mentioned before that I had been seeking peace of mind to the point that I had scheduled almost every minute of each day, striving to be better than I was the day before but finding no real calm or everlasting peace when the day was done. My faith was what turned the tide. Slowly, I noticed my inner critic quieting down. I worried less. I felt more grateful for what I had. The deeper I grew in my faith—the closer I felt to Christ—the more I found the calm I'd been looking for. I came to accept that someone had my back and that, at the end of each day, I was exactly where He wanted me to be.

My story is not unique. Faith can have some big-time positive effects on people, including finding that same calm I'd discovered. So let's break down just a few of the areas where a spiritual practice can have a positive effect on our lives.

---

15   https://www.washingtonpost.com/national/religion/religion-is-a-sure-route-to-true-happiness/2014/01/23/f6522120-8452-11e3-bbe5-6a2a3141e3a9_story.html?noredirect=on&utm_term=.77326702b0c1

PEACE OF MIND

Several of the studies I alluded to previously talk about religion as it relates to stress. And it turns out that people who are part of a religious community are less stressed out than most, which is huge! Stress can be a major detractor from our sense of happiness, and it also has some pretty nasty side effects on our health.

So what is it about religion that eases stress? A couple of things actually.

First, we often turn to faith in times when we need support. Maybe you're going through a hard time or are hoping to land that dream job, so you go back to church for some comfort or ask someone to say a little prayer for you. Religious organizations and groups often play a major role as support systems for their congregants.

In fact, it's been shown that people who regularly attend religious services tend to have larger social networks and feel more supported by those networks.[16] Did you really need any more proof that your network is your net worth? But there it is again, the idea that the people you surround yourself with can have an enormous impact on your happiness. In this case, they may help you through tough times and provide support when you need it, easing your overall stress.

The second way religion can help ease stress is by providing you with the knowledge that you aren't alone. Yes, you've got your fellow church-goers. But in most religions, you also have a higher power that you can speak to directly. Prayer can provide enormous comfort. It can help you talk through your feelings on a topic. It can help you vocalize what's most important to you. And it's a constant reminder that there's a higher power on the receiving end who has your back.

---

16   http://spirituality.ucla.edu/docs/newsletters/4/idler_final.pdf

ETHICAL GUIDANCE

Have you ever been faced with a decision that made your stomach turn? You didn't know the right answer or something felt off. Your gut was telling you something. In moments of indecision, faith can provide you with guidance, helping you figure out how to behave.

I know what you're thinking. *Yes, Aaron, we remember the WWJD bracelets.*

(That's "What Would Jesus Do?" for those of who don't remember.)

Thinking about what Jesus would do in a given situation isn't a bad idea—in fact, it's something I always try to consider. But I'm talking about something bigger. I'm talking about making sure that all of your actions line up with your personal values, and faith can really help you to define those values. For centuries, we have relied on religion as our moral compass, and many religions share the same guiding principles.

While some may specifically forbid alcohol or eating certain meats, almost all of them talk about treating other people with kindness, cherishing the body and life you've been given, and practicing gratitude and grace. Some of the same things we've already been talking about, right?

When you're not sure about something, your faith may serve as a helpful reminder to point you on the right path forward. In fact, it's been shown that faith can make a huge difference to participants in Alcoholics Anonymous. Of the 12 steps in the program, 8 of them mention God. And according to *The Power of Habit*, those who embrace the religious aspects of the program have a higher chance of staying sober. The author credits that fact to the participants having something higher to stay sober for and something that reminds them of the greater rewards of their hard work.

So in some ways, faith can reinforce some commonly held ethical values, but it can also provide you with a larger context for *why* you should behave in a certain way. What is waiting for you at the end of your life? What kinds of actions may prevent you from a deeper relationship with

God? What are the Fruits of the Spirit you'll receive by following your church's ethical guidelines?

QUALITY OF LIFE

The Blue Zones was a groundbreaking book when it came out. Author Dan Buettner spent years studying communities with high populations of centenarians, or people who have lived to be 100 or more years old. In addition to some of the assumed qualities of these communities, like naturally active lifestyles and mostly plant-based diets, these "blue zones" have another thing in common: belonging.

The overwhelming majority of centenarians interviewed belonged to a religious community. And according to the Blue Zones website, "Research shows that attending faith-based services four times per month will add 4-14 years of life expectancy."[17]

Why is that, you may ask. There are a few theories out there, but one is that most religions support moderation, if not abstaining entirely, from things that may be harmful to the body, like alcohol or certain foods. Most religions incorporate some form of fasting into their practice. Raised Catholic, I certainly remember cutting out meat on Fridays during lent or giving something up that I enjoyed for 40 days. When we deny ourselves things that would otherwise bring pleasure, we're practicing self-control. We're less likely to overeat or drink to excess. We stay away from riskier behaviors in general.

There's also the idea that the people we surround ourselves with make us better. One of my favorite phrases originates from the Bible, fittingly enough, and reads, "As iron sharpens iron, so one person sharpens another (Proverbs 27:17)."

According again to the Blue Zones website, "Research from the

---

17   https://www.bluezones.com/2016/11/power-9/

Framingham Studies shows that smoking, obesity, happiness, and even loneliness are contagious. So the social networks of long-lived people have favorably shaped their health behaviors."

All of that is to say that when we are surrounded by a community that shares some similar values with us, they will inevitably help us live those values more fully. Because so many of our values may align with or come from religious communities, it's difficult to think of another place where we might go to find so many like-minded, supportive people in one place.

How does all of that sound? Pretty wonderful, right? Who wouldn't want to live longer and be surrounded by people who sharpen you and make you better? If you're on board to at least give it a try, next I'm going to share how to get started. And if you're currently practicing a faith, these same ideas will help you to grow deeper in that faith and, hopefully, radiate joy as a result.

FINDING FAITH

Before we jump into any specific ideas for finding and growing in faith, there's one small prerequisite. And I think you know what I'm talking about—vulnerability. It's going to be key here. So as you explore some of the suggestions coming up or as you're taking on some of the daily challenges, try to go at it from a place of openness and curiosity. Allow yourself to speak freely about what you're thinking and feeling. Ask questions, of others and of yourself. And give yourself some time and breathing room to think.

And if you're completely unclear about where to start, I invite you to join me in my own Christian faith and see how you like it. In the coming sections, I share more about my journey to faith and details of how I practice, so following in those footsteps can be a great place to begin.

A friend recently asked me why Christianity focuses so much on spreading the faith to others. Why not just practice your own faith and leave others be, she wondered.

My feelings are that when God fills you up, you should share that love with others, not in an attempt to add followers to the church's ranks for the sake of adding followers but in order to have a positive impact on their lives. Think of a lamp in a dark room. The point of the lamp is not to be covered up, its light kept secret. Rather, it's intended to fill a room with brightness and light. When I feel filled by Christ's love, I don't want to hide it and keep it to myself. I want to be that lamp, sharing what I feel with those around me. And so, out of love for my own faith, I invite you to join me and share in the light with me. And it is simply that—an invitation.

FIND A MENTOR, GURU, GUIDE, FRIEND

The chances are high that there are also some spiritual "lamps" in your existing network who love their faith and would be thrilled to talk about it. Having conversations about your faith allows you to go a little deeper, answer questions you hadn't considered, and get someone else's perspective on the matter.

But if that's not something you already do regularly, or maybe if you don't have an existing church community to turn to, start by considering people in your immediate network that you admire. Is there anyone you feel comfortable talking about faith with? Is there anyone who seems to take real joy in their faith?

If not, it may be time to embrace some change and meet new folks. Identify people that are strong believers and seek out their advice. Ask about what guides their life and why they live the way they do.

It's important when looking for a potential mentor in faith to find someone that will be totally accepting of your vulnerability and who will be vulnerable in return. The goal isn't to find someone who will dictate what and how to believe but rather to find someone who will openly share their own personal belief system. That often means more than just sharing some key Bible passages; it means talking about their struggles, their joys, their questions. It means discussion and shared knowledge. Talk to a few different people, and, in combination with your own research and experimentation, they may help point you in the direction that's right for you.

And if you're looking to grow in your current faith more, seek out people who may fill in your own personal gaps. For instance, when Joslyn and I met, she was way more versed in the scriptures. She could quote entire passages, and when I had questions about what specific readings meant, she was the first person I went to. I, on the other hand, was often able to internalize some of the church's teachings, like forgiveness, more easily. So when Joslyn felt annoyed or hurt by someone, she came to me to talk it through and find encouragement.

Remember also that faith is a lifetime practice. If you find a church that you love, that's wonderful. But regular thought, introspection, and discussions with people who will challenge and deepen your beliefs will allow you to discover more depths to your own faith than you knew possible.

When I met my mentor, my spiritual life began to flourish, growing from the seeds my mother planted into a continually budding tree. And I am forever grateful for both.

Write down 3 people you admire and could reach out to for a discussion about their faith and values.

_____

_____

_____

_____

PUT YOURSELF IN THE RIGHT SITUATIONS

You'd be hard-pressed to find more like-minded people in one room than at a church that's the right fit for you. But beyond trying out different church services every weekend to find the one that feels right, there are other ways to find like-minded people—people who may be the kinds of friends and mentors we just talked about.

If it's important to you to grow in your faith and to adopt some of its values, there are plenty of activities and groups you can join where you're likely to find people who share those same values. If being a better Christian, for example, is really important to you, as it is for me, then you *know* that a bar where everyone is drinking heavily isn't the right place to be. Neither is hanging out with that group of friends who only seem to want to talk badly about anyone who's not there. Your gut will tell you when you're not in the right environment for you and when the people you've surrounded yourself with just don't share the same values.

Change can be scary, but do your best to force yourself into some new situations. Instead of going to a happy hour that you know will turn into a mean-spirited gossip session, join a sports league. Go for a hike. Go to a coffee shop and read a book. Put yourself in situations where the people you're interacting with at least stand a chance at being a positive force in your life. They may not always. But if you know that your regular social situations aren't going to support your values, don't keep repeating them and hoping for different results.

There's a famous quote, widely attributed to Albert Einstein, that says, "The definition of insanity is doing the same thing over and over again and expecting different results." If you keep putting yourself in situations that you know violate your personal values, then eventually your values may change. Behaviors and attitudes are contagious, and negative ones have the potential to rub off on you, too. Is it more important to you that you not upset anyone by backing off a toxic friendship than it is to make room for relationships that fill you up? That make you better?

Your relationships are everything, and it's up to you to surround your-self with the right people. To do that, put yourself in the right situations to meet them. Trust your gut.

Quickly jot down the activities you do and places you go where you feel you are living out your values. Where do you feel right? Where are you when your gut tells you something bad?

DO YOUR RESEARCH

When it comes to finding the faith that's right for you, there's an abso-lutely overwhelming number of options. Even within Christianity, you've got Catholic, Methodist, Presbyterian, Baptist, Episcopalian, Adventist, and nondenominational faiths. And within any one of those are several different churches, each with their own pastor or priest, their own cul-ture, their own personality.

When it comes to religion, we rarely question "what" we are. I was raised Catholic, and when I was in college, I told people I was Catholic, even while feeling very distant from the church. (Nowadays, I would be a little broader and tell folks I'm a Christian.) Oftentimes, what we were raised to believe seems like the only option. And with that comes the feel-ing that our childhood church must be a representation of all churches in the faith. It feels like, surely, they're all just the same. But even within one faith, each church and congregation can *feel* very different. The key is to not get lost in the minutiae of how one faith is different from another but to focus on fostering a relationship with God, putting yourself in the atmosphere that will best help you do that.

So even if you feel strongly in your overall faith and just need some kind of a change, try out a few different services. See if a new environment or new pastor makes a difference for you. And if you feel completely disconnected from faith, allow yourself, even if just for a short time, to forget about what you were raised to be. I know that it's important to some families that everyone believe the same thing, and believing something else could have some serious repercussions, like disappointing certain family members. But that's getting ahead of ourselves. For now, just allow yourself to get a better understanding of what faith truly is.

Start big and read up on the commonly practiced faiths of today. What are the major differences between them? What are the similarities? Talk to people from different faiths and try to get an understanding of what it is that drives their faith.

Allow your Mental Pillar practice to help you out. Be curious about faith. And try to get a sense for which big-picture option feels right to you. From there, start to whittle down even further. If you were raised Protestant, do you really know the difference between Protestant and Episcopalian? Find out. Start to get a little more granular in your search and feel out what's right for you. It's important that, while you do research and ask questions, you also stay connected to your emotions and heart.

In that sense, finding the right faith is a lot like buying a house. A friend of mine recently told me how he and his wife were convinced they'd found the right house for them. Everything about the online listing was perfect—the number of bedrooms, the backyard space, the finishes. When they went to see it in person, something felt off. They sat in the house for almost an hour, trying to convince themselves they loved it as much as they thought they would.

Their realtor suggested then that they go peek at a house down the street that was also for sale. They could pop in just to compare the two and maybe get some perspective on why the first house felt off.

When they got to house number two, it took five minutes for them to realize it was exactly what they had been looking for. There was just *something* about it. They put an offer on it that night.

I share that story to say that, while you can read all about every modern religion till you retire, there's no substitute for going and experiencing it in real life. When you walk in, it will feel right or it won't. There's no use convincing yourself that you "are" a certain religion when something is off. So give yourself the freedom and grace to explore. And just go.

Write down a few questions you have about faith. What are you curious about? What doesn't make sense to you? Try to seek out the answers over the next few days.

AN ATTITUDE OF GRATITUDE

Remember when you were a kid and you found a lucky penny? It was the best day. It was like the whole universe was working together to bring you luck. And every good thing that happened after finding the penny? Well, it was all due to your newfound luck, of course.

One of the joys of things like lucky pennies is that they remind us to pay attention and to look for the good. As kids, we were way more likely to notice small good things, like the ice cream truck coming that day or a butterfly landing on us, if we'd found that penny.

When we get older, we ask instead for signs from God. We think, if

God is real, I'll get that job or He'll send me the perfect partner. We begin looking for the signs we want, rather than accepting and feeling grateful for the signs He sends.

When growing deeper in your faith, keep an eye out for small, everyday miracles. Think back to your work in the Emotional Pillar and find the good in every situation. Turn your attention away from asking for the things you think you want and toward recognizing the great things you've already been sent.

By doing so, you'll experience real, repeated connection with God, which will fuel your desire to explore your faith more. There are so many small miracles that could be meaningful to only you, if only you stopped to take notice. Every day, there's a sunset. Every day, there's nature to enjoy. Every day, there's an opportunity to recognize all that you've accomplished and all that you've been given, instead of focusing only on what comes next.

Write down 3 things that you are grateful for at this moment. What are the first things that come to mind? What small miracles did you witness today?

FORGIVE AND FORGET

Forgiveness is a key practice in most faiths, but what I'm referring to here extends to forgiving yourself. No matter which faith you practice, you will never be a perfect disciple of it. And that's completely okay.

A friend of mine struggled with exactly that, and it affected his ability to go deeper in his faith. One day when we were chatting, he told me how down on himself he'd been feeling. He felt like everything he did was a sin and that he was constantly praying for forgiveness. The guilt of his small, everyday sins started to add up, making religion feel like a chore, rather than a joy. It felt like punishment.

Then I asked him, "You're asking forgiveness from God, but do you then grant forgiveness to yourself?"

It was like a lightbulb went off for him, and he realized that he wasn't allowing himself any grace for simply being human. When he asked forgiveness for his sins, he wasn't really wiping his slate clean. Rather, he was keeping a running tally of all the ways he thought he'd screwed up. And that running tally began to weigh on him.

Without forgiving yourself for your mistakes, it's easy to spiral. You may question what the point is for all the prayer and church services and scripture studies. But when you do grant yourself forgiveness, the pressure to become perfect all the time lessens and an understanding grows that your spirituality is a lifelong journey to become better. A little closer to perfect, while realizing that true perfection is an impossible goal. By not beating yourself up, you will be able to find more joy in faith.

List 3 things you did recently that you wish you hadn't. In writing them down, grant yourself forgiveness for those actions.

PRAYER TAKES PRACTICE

Finally, my last suggestion for establishing and growing in your faith is a simple one—pray.

When I first got back into the habit of going to church regularly, prayer was surprisingly difficult. I didn't know what to say. I was way out of practice. So I started off just by talking about my day. In the back of my mind I thought, *Am I boring God? What do other people talk to Him about?*

Over time, my prayers became like therapy sessions. I opened up little by little about things that were bothering me, things I was excited about, what I hoped for the people in my life. My thoughts and emotions just started bubbling to the surface without much effort, and I found my rhythm. But it took some time.

Prayer is, hands down, the easiest way to deepen your faith. All you have to do is talk. And even if you're not sure if someone is listening on the other side (or you're concerned that what you have to say isn't interesting), you'll eventually begin to feel a presence there. You won't feel like you're talking to the walls in your room for long.

And the beautiful thing about it? That presence then begins to come with you through your day. You start to send up quick prayers whenever you need to talk. It becomes a part of your routine, a habit. And you stop feeling so alone.

It's also great practice for speaking your hopes and dreams aloud. What we pray for most often is what we'd like to see happen in our lives. In other words, we pray to accomplish our goals. And talking about your goals out loud is an important first step in achieving them because you acknowledge how much they mean to you. Maybe you're not ready to share them with friends and family quite yet. Share them with God first. Keep in mind that God doesn't always answer our prayers the way we'd prefer. He has an ultimate plan for our lives that is far greater than what we sometimes imagine for ourselves.

Don't know where to start or what to say? Start there. Tell God that you don't know what to say. Talk about your day. Talk about the weather. Talk about your relationships. Tell Him what you're hoping will happen that day. Tell Him what you hope for your spouse or parents or kids. Tell Him what you're struggling with.

Just start talking.

And keep talking.

Jot down 3 things you're hoping for right now. Good weather this weekend? A new friend to come into your life? Whatever it is, be honest and put it in writing here.

Your faith can—and should be—a joy-filled journey. Keep that in mind as you explore it further. I will always think about my mom when I was growing up and the smile that was on her face every time we walked into mass. That's what I strive to feel for myself.

Faith allows us to feel a deeper connection with life, with the planet, and with the people around us. It gives us a context for why we exist. It provides us with a supportive, kind community. And once we find the right path, it has the potential to fill us to the brim with joy.

That is what I hope for you, too.

I think back to the seeds my mom planted in us kids in childhood through her openness, her joy, and her support. Over time, some of those many seeds took root in me, and continue to bud into an ever-growing tree, the wind carrying new seeds to those who need them.

Maybe you're not ready to dive headfirst into faith. That's okay. You are exactly where you're supposed to be. Keep this book and this chapter in the back of your mind. Let it be the seed that you come back to when you're ready. When that time comes, you'll open your eyes to a new world and you'll know.

With that, we're about to move into our last Pillar. Are you ready? Next up, we're talking about our professional lives and how to make sure that what you do with the majority of your waking hours lines up with your values. Work is a huge time commitment, so let's make sure we're using that time wisely.

CHAPTER 7

THE PROFESSIONAL PILLAR

"Opportunity is missed by most people because
it is dressed in overalls and looks like work."

–THOMAS A. EDISON

WHAT IS A MENTOR? Given how much we've talked about mentors already, I'll admit it's a little late to start defining the word. But the reason I've waited until now is because when we hear the term mentor thrown around in everyday conversation, our minds may immediately go to someone in a suit, sharing years of hard-won business wisdom over coffee or drinks. In other words, we often have a very narrow, specific idea of what mentorship looks like.

We've already seen over the course of this book how that can be different. We should be on the lookout for people who could be spiritual mentors, emotional mentors, physical mentors, and so on. You get the idea. In every area of our lives, we can—and should—look to people who do it better or have things more figured out to improve.

That includes seeking out professional mentors. But what I don't want to happen is, once we start talking about our professional lives, to revert back to that old idea of what a mentor is. Maybe you'll find that perfect guru who can lift you up in all areas of your professional life, and maybe you'll meet and talk about it over drinks while wearing suits.

In reality, mentorship just means the sharing of knowledge and wisdom from one person to another. They are often trusted advisors who share perspective and lessons they've learned. It's a relationship that can evolve from anything, and it's that simple.

But if your experience is anything like mine, you won't have just one professional mentor. And you'll never find someone who can lift you up in *every* single aspect of your professional life.

The closest person I have to that kind of mentor has been my dad. He raised me, so he's been mentoring me since day one. He taught me how to be respectful and kind to people. He taught me how to stand up for myself. He taught me what belonged on a resume and what didn't. For years, my dad helped me build a foundation of professional skills that I put to use in college and beyond.

When I was a little older, his role changed. We started talking about investing. He got me interested in real estate and the opportunity it creates. He instilled in me the idea that I should make money work for me, that I shouldn't work for money.

Far and away, he's had the biggest impact on my professional success. But he wasn't alone.

When I went into insurance, I worked out at the gym with my boss every morning, and he gave me priceless advice about the industry. He helped me understand the ins and outs of it and create my place within it.

When I became interested in performance and leadership coaching, I found mentors there, too. I sought out people who had done it before.

I enrolled in Jairek Robbins' training program and learned about the science behind our beliefs and actions.

When Joslyn and I started a realty company to help other people buy, sell, and invest in property, we relied on some knowledge I'd gained from my dad and built onto it by reaching out to established realtors.

Looking back, I can see how all of these people had an influence on different areas of my professional life. And I have a lot to learn still! So I'll continue to seek out these moments of "micro-mentorship," as I've started calling them.

Micro-mentorship simply means the small (or sometimes big), life-changing relationships that help you grow, sharpen your abilities, and help you reach your max potential. They can be people you keep in touch with for years or a simple conversation over coffee. Together, they add up to so much more.

Everyone I've talked to about mentorship has said the same thing— that it's rare to find a single mentor who can help you achieve *all* of your goals. So how about we stop trying?

To expect so much of one person not only creates some unrealistic expectations (and a lot of pressure for your desired mentor), but it also undercuts the breadth of your professional life. I am a big believer that your professional life includes a lot more than your day job. It includes your investments, passive income streams, entrepreneurial endeavors, and whatever else you do to create financial freedom.

And that's the goal, really. We work so we can have money. We hope to make money in a way that fulfills us. But I want more for you than a job. I want you to have the peace of mind to know that if something happens to that job, you'll be okay.

THE GOAL IS FINANCIAL FREEDOM

I came across an interesting article not long ago that said only 39% of Americans had enough money in savings to cover a $1,000 emergency, like a car breaking down or the A/C going out. Think about that. A big chunk of Americans would be forced to borrow money to cover an expense like that, rather than paying for it out of pocket.

Now imagine if it were worse than the A/C breaking. You lose your job, get a hole in your roof, or worse yet, get really sick. The debt could be crippling and extremely difficult to pull yourself out of, but that's how so many of us are living. No matter how many new cars and trips to Bali we see on our social feeds, the reality is that so many Americans are not financially stable.

When we were young and in school, adults told us that one day we'd grow up, get an education, find a job, live comfortably, and retire. It sounded simple, and it certainly motivated many of us to work hard in school and seek out high-paying jobs after graduation.

But even with that groundwork laid out for us, one thing few adults explained to us was how to save and how to live within our means. As a result, there's a large divide among Millennials when it comes to saving. According to one recent study, 66% of Millennials have no retirement savings whatsoever. According to another, 1 in 6 Millennials has over $100,000 in savings.

In other words, some of us are killing it while others are letting the best years to save go by. My goal in writing this section isn't to applaud those who are doing great and move on. It's also not to give you a light pep talk and hope it sticks. If something bad does happen, I want you to be ready for it. Even better, I want you to live the life of your dreams. I want to change the conversation away from thinking that after that next promotion, everything will be better.

Financial freedom doesn't just mean making more money. If you get a promotion and have more expendable income, that's great. But it's not the end goal. Let's spend a little more time talking about what financial freedom means and why it matters.

DEFINING FINANCIAL FREEDOM

There are a lot of definitions of financial freedom out there in the world. I began reconsidering what I thought it meant after reading *Rich Dad, Poor Dad* by Robert Kiyosaki (thanks for the recommendation, Dad), and it's this definition that has stuck with me.

He says that wealth is not about how much money you make, but rather about how much money you keep. For many of us, once the paycheck comes in, we think, *Yes, now I can buy that new TV.* The money is flying out of the account as quickly as it came in.

Kiyosaki's philosophy, however, says that if you want a new TV, you should spend your paycheck on something that will generate enough income for you to afford it. In other words, instead of letting your paycheck dictate the lifestyle you can afford, you should live modestly, invest in things that will make money for you, and use that additional income on the things you want but don't need. To me, it was a totally new way to think about money.

Tony Robbins' definition of financial freedom is much more rooted in our own mindsets. It's about feeling truly alive and grateful for what you have. He pushes folks to figure out what makes them feel full of abundance and then to find ways to make sure that everything in that lifestyle is covered, without needing to work.

I like both of these definitions because they force you to start with a clear idea of what it is you want in life. In that sense, they are spot on. My own definition of financial freedom builds on that and reads:

Financial freedom means earning enough passive income to live according to your values and achieve your goals without fear or reliance on an employer as your only income source.

I think it's important to mention values in our definition because within the financial industry, images of Porsches and yachts and private jets are all over the place. But you don't have to want or have the traditional symbols of wealth to be financially free. In fact, there's a big difference between being rich and being financially free.

A rich person may make a lot of money and spend a lot of money, leaving little left over at the end of the day. A person who's achieved financial freedom knows that they have enough money left to cover the lifestyle they want.

And what you want can be as simple as not being terrified of a medical emergency bankrupting you. It can be paying for the college your child wants to attend. It can be going on a trip once a year. Or it can be a Porsche. It's totally up to you.

If you start by thinking about what you really want in your life, it gives your money a purpose. It's about putting money to use to drive your own happiness. It's important as you explore different ways to find financial freedom that you remember it all ties back to your why. Without that, you'll be trapped in a cycle of thinking that happiness will be found behind your next big purchase.

(Hint: You'll never find it there.)

UNDERSTANDING YOUR WHY

Money can't buy happiness. We've all heard that before. But while more money doesn't necessarily mean more happiness, the two ideas are in fact linked. If you are scared every time a bill comes, you're probably not feeling fulfilling joy. You've got a weight on your shoulders that limits your happiness.

More than that, if you aren't able to do the things that bring you real joy because of money concerns, your happiness is limited again. You may value your family above all else. But if you're not able to spend time with them because you're working 90-hour weeks, are you happy?

Change is incremental. If you want to spend more time with your family, quitting your job may put the family's future and stability at risk. So if you're struggling to get by, it doesn't feel like an option.

But if you start with an awareness of your values, you can make small and incremental changes that will help you get to a place of happiness eventually. Using this same example, you might think that if you can't spend time with your kids, you may as well treat them to the new XBox they've been asking for. You may not be there to watch them play with it, but maybe you buying it for them will make up for that fact.

But again, if your personal value is family, how does that expensive purchase help you get closer to them? Will you regret that they didn't have an XBox ten years from now? Or will you regret not putting that money into a savings account to help you start a business that will allow you to work from home and spend more time with them?

There is no right or wrong answer about how to spend the money you earn, particularly when you have a family that's dependent on it. The only point I'm trying to make here is that every dollar holds some power. It can bring you closer to your personal values or pull you further from them. When you weigh your spending choices, think of them in the context of your personal values and goals—your "why."

A friend recently asked me how to find balance in that choice. "Does every penny go toward my goals?" he asked.

In other words, should he live like a hermit now to have everything he wants a decade from now, or should he enjoy his life now and save moderately for the future? How aggressive should he be in seeking financial freedom?

It's a difficult line to walk, and my suggestion is to ask yourself how much happier you'd be if you made that purchase. Someone who loves to travel should consider how much happier they'd be taking five trips this year instead of one. Is it exponentially more?

Someone buying a house should ask how much happier they'll be with the extra room and bathroom. Does it mean you'll be able to host more friends? Does that bring you joy? Or do you want it because it feels like you *should* want the bigger, more expensive house?

We're almost never faced with a black-and-white financial decision. To buy or not to buy. Rather, it's more often a choice between many, many options. You can buy from the top shelf, the bargain barrel, or anywhere in between. When considering a more expensive option, is the increase in joy proportional to the increased price? The answer to that will always come back to your values. Let the driving forces in your life influence even the small decisions, and you'll see it pay off (literally) down the road.

That's a lot about spending habits. So if you're wondering how it fits into a chapter about professional fulfillment, it's because our professional goals are so often centered around income. Few of us really want the promotion because we *want* to work longer hours. Sure, we may like the power or the new responsibilities. But the honest-to-goodness truth is that most of us want the promotion because we want the paycheck.

So if we change up our ideas about spending, or pushing out the money that's coming in, we open ourselves up for new goals. How else can we use the money we earn to achieve the life we want? How else can we obtain financial freedom beyond relying on that promotion?

We'll get to what those other goals can be soon, but for now, let's focus on changing our thinking about our professions a bit. The day job, the career, the profession, whatever you want to call it, is our foundation. On top of that, we build a secure structure that will protect us in case of tough times or stormy weather. And there's a lot to be gained from a strong foundation.

TRADITIONAL AREAS OF PROFESSIONAL FULFILLMENT

While it's nice to think of ourselves as entrepreneurs with passive incomes big enough to fund summering in the French countryside, the reality is that most will be in traditional employment roles. At least for now.

But while I don't think relying on a nine-to-five for both fulfillment and financial stability is the best choice in the long run, there is a lot of be gained from a steady job. So I will encourage you to explore some other income streams like investing or side hustles, but continue looking for (or enjoying, if you've found one) a job that fills you up.

After all, we spend the majority of our waking hours at work. We should enjoy it, right? So when it comes to our baseline, foundational income, here are a few things to look out for.

RELATIONSHIP BUILDING

You've got your work friends, your school friends, your sports friends, and so on. But as you get older, the lines between friend groups can start to blur. You may want to spend more time with work friends, outside of the occasional happy hour or quick lunch. Maybe you invite them to join your book club or to meet some other friends.

For many of us, work can be one of the best sources of new friends. And if having several strong relationships fills you up, it may be important to you that your work environment be conducive to bonding.

If you're interested in going to the office, doing your work, collecting a paycheck, and going home, then maybe it's less important to you that your office offer perks like a full spread of food for lunch or fun monthly staff outings.

Whatever your preference, the opportunity for relationship building can have a big effect on your overall happiness in a company. So be honest about what you're looking for (there's no shame in wanting a quiet office with regular hours), and pay attention when interviewing for new positions to the kinds of initiatives the company has in place to shape their culture.

PLAYING TO YOUR STRENGTHS

Sometimes it just feels good to do something that you're good at. I understand business and investing, and when I talk about it, I feel good about my expertise.

If you're naturally talkative and personable, then sitting in a cubicle and only sending emails all day every day may be a waste of your natural skills and talents.

Maybe you studied English and are a strong writer. Creating reports and spending all your time in Excel may not fill you up.

Or even if you're an everlasting optimist, simply being around negative people could zap your energy over time.

We all have natural and learned aptitudes, but we don't always prioritize them when applying for jobs. We think about what will make us more money in the long run, what will pay the bills *now*, or what our parents would prefer we do. But doing what you are good at *feels good*. So whether you get your fill of it through a hobby or a side hustle instead of your full-time job, finding a way to play to your strengths is a surefire way to avoid burnout out from a job that may not come naturally.

Don't forget to consider the things you'd like to be good at, too. What goals do you have? What skills would you like to learn? Will your current position help to get you there? It's not all about resting on your laurels but also about pushing yourself to new heights. When it comes to your personal skill set, adding new talents and knowledge should ideally be done with intention.

In other words, your jobs don't shape the skills you learn. You pick the jobs to gain or hone the skills you want. Remember, you can't spell challenge without change, and change does not occur in your comfort zone. Get outside of it. Push yourself to new limits.

YOUR TIME

Is your job a classic nine-to-five with an hour for lunch? Or are the lines between your personal and professional life completely blurred? Are you always "on"?

For some jobs, that kind of work-life flow is just a fact of life. Maybe you're self-employed and bill by the hour. In that case, the more you work, the more you make. It can be incredibly tempting to wear yourself thin trying to squeeze in just one more job.

But whether you are in complete control of your schedule or are at the beck and call of a manager, spend some time thinking about how much personal time you need to decompress. Are you able to quickly answer an email on your phone after hours without it throwing off your downtime? Or would you prefer to have clean breaks between work time and personal time?

We've talked already about the immense pressure our society puts on employees to always be "on." But when your well-being is at stake, it's worth making sure that doing so isn't causing you undue stress. That stress will also rub off on the people around you if you aren't careful. So look for a job that allows the right balance of time commitment for you. And if you're the boss, try to set some clear rules and boundaries for yourself to protect your personal time.

MISSION

Almost every company has a mission statement. In the next chapter, we're also going to create our own personal mission statements. Every so often, we may luck into a situation where our employer's mission state-ment lines up nicely with our own.

In that case, there's a tremendous opportunity to find fulfillment through your work because you know you will be living out your values. If you work for a nonprofit helping to supply clean water to third-world nations and your own mission is to be a force of positive change in the world, then you may just walk into work each day knowing that you are making a difference. And that will feel fantastic.

A lot of the times when my own friends talk about being inspired by their company's mission, it's often said as a justification for long hours or small paychecks. In other words, they tell me that the trade-off is worth it because they are able to live out their values.

Finding fulfillment through the mission of your company can be absolutely worth some sacrifices. It's a pretty rare achievement, after all. But those trade-offs are exactly why your primary employment shouldn't be the only aspect of your professional life. It's possible to help people, for example, and still be financially comfortable through smart investments. In fact, it may help you to help even more people down the road.

FINANCIAL COMFORT

Last but not least, there are the jobs that give us a healthy paycheck. This is the kind of job that so many of us seem to be striving to find. If we can just make a little more, we'll be able to afford more and be happy. We won't have to worry about bills. We won't have to worry about keeping up with the Joneses. Heck, we'll be the Joneses.

The truth of the matter is that sometimes these kinds of jobs do fill us up and make us happy. But sometimes they require long hours and drain our energy. And when we do get the increase in pay, our lifestyle stan-dards increase with it. So we're left striving for more and more money.

Don't get me wrong. A high-paying job can open a lot of doors and give us more options for how to spend our money. I bring up the common pitfalls to remind ourselves that, if the only thing we're getting from employment is money, we'll need to be careful with what you use that money for later on. We need to be intentional with our spending to make up for the lack of fulfillment work brings. We need to use the personal time available to us to engage with life, to do what drives us, what fills us with energy. What, beyond the paycheck, will energize you to return to work on Monday morning?

At the end of the day, you're likely to spend a considerable amount of your life working. To some, the ability to work and support themselves provides all the professional fulfillment they'll need. Others want more from their professional lives. They want to feel like the time they're spending every day on work is worth it—that they get something from it in return. That may be lasting friendships or a connection to a company's cause. Whatever it is, I encourage you to look out for opportunities to enrich your professional life, first by setting yourself up with an employer that's the right fit for *you* and then by exploring some less traditional professional opportunities, too.

OTHER PROFESSIONAL PATHWAYS TO CONSIDER

So what are these less traditional opportunities? We've talked about a few, like investing and real estate, already, both of which I'm a huge believer in. There are many other ways to diversify your income in addition to these. Some may be more accessible to you than others, depending on where you are in your professional and financial journey. But they all follow the same basic principle: **Make money work for you; don't work for your money.**

All of these options start by taking money that you earn through income and investing it in ways that will pay you back, plus a little extra. In other words, they will do more for you than simply putting 100% of your extra income into savings and letting it accumulate.

And the great thing about it is that, no matter your current financial state, you can still do something to grow your income more. We'll start small and work our way up to some larger opportunities. Do what's right for you, but whatever you do, don't write off the idea of investing completely. Even if you're only contributing a few dollars a month, do *something* to help set yourself up for a more secure future.

INVESTING

401(K)

Start with the basics. Most companies these days offer some kind of retirement savings account, the most common being the 401(k) plan. If you happen to be with a company that offers a matching program, meaning if you put a percentage of your income into that account the company will do the same, then you're in luck. Starting a 401(k) account is one of the easiest ways to get started with investing.

But there are a surprising number of people who don't take advantage of this option, especially among Millennials. Not only is the company giving you free money, but the earlier you start getting money in your account, the more time it has to grow. So why would so many Millennials turn down that offer?

The most common answer I've heard is that they can't afford it. They need 100% of their paycheck to be able to live. And to that I say, is that really true? If you're being completely honest with yourself, are you really budgeting every dollar and cent and still coming up short? Or are you buying what you want without the help of a budget and realizing later that there's nothing left?

If the second scenario is the case, I'd be willing to bet that you could start putting away 1% of your paycheck into a 401(k) account without noticing a thing. After a month or two of doing that, you could probably up your contribution to 2%, again without much pain. There is no rule that says that if your company matches up to 4%, you should contribute that right away. Start where you feel comfortable, but make it a goal to work up to the max your company will match. Otherwise, you really are just turning down free money.

And that money can do wonders the more time it has in your account. For example, let's imagine that you started saving $200 per month at age 25. Your coworker also began saving $200 per month but did so starting at age 35. If you both keep saving until 65 years old, it makes sense that you would have more in the bank than your coworker. With that additional time, you will have personally put in 33% more money from your regular contributions. But with the benefit of compound interest, which helps enhance those contributions year over year, you will be left with almost twice as much money at retirement than your coworker.[18]

And all because it sat in your bank account for longer.

So if you don't have a retirement savings account, the best time to start one is now. You can't do anything about the past, but the sooner you start saving for your future, the more prepared you'll be. Start small if you need to, but just get started.

IRA

So what if your company doesn't offer a 401(k)? You're not alone, unfortunately. A recent study found that 35% of private sector workers over

18   https://www.businessinsider.com/saving-at-25-vs-saving-at-35-2014-3

the age of 22 aren't offered a 401(k) plan. But does this mean that your chances for retiring at a reasonable age are shot?

Absolutely not! While 401(k)'s are the most prevalent and talked about retirement savings option, there are others that you can take advantage of no matter where you work. Have you heard of an IRA? The term literally means Individual Retirement Account, and it's meant for people to put post-tax money into these accounts to plan for retirement.

I won't get too deep in the weeds here, but the main way an IRA differs from a 401(k) has to do with taxes. In other words, are you contributing money that was taxed when you earned it (IRA) or that will be taxed when you withdraw it in retirement (401[k]). In general, it's a good idea to have both accounts, since we have no idea what the tax rate will be in the future. So if you're company offers a plan, start there. Then check out what your bank offers and look into having a few accounts.

These kinds of basic retirement accounts should be your first move when looking beyond your paycheck to generate income. Don't think of contributing to them every month as optional. This should just be part of your professional life now.

INDEX FUNDS

Once you've got those bricks laid, you can start looking into some other investing options. When you start talking about the stock market, there are seemingly endless ways to get involved. It can be overwhelming. You can buy bonds, invest in CDs or mutual funds, or try your hand at investing in individual stocks. But if I've found one thing to be true, it's that investing in index funds are one of the safest, simplest ways to get involved in the stock market.

An index fund is essentially a grouping of companies. When you put money in an index fund, you are hoping that the overall trend of those companies together will be positive. So one company may tank, but if the rest can carry its weight, you won't lose money. The one we hear about most often is the S&P 500 Index, which is a grouping of 500 companies. And you know what? It consistently does better than what hedge fund managers are able to make for their clients, broadly speaking.

That's because, as time goes by, the market continues to improve, slowly but surely. Sure, there may be some dips here and there. The news may panic and yell recession, but remember that, especially if you're in your 20s and 30s, the market will rebound eventually. It will come back stronger. So resist the urge to withdraw your money when there are blips, slumps, recessions, and so on. Play the long game instead, and think about yourself at 65.

An important note to make here is that you can often elect to have your 401(k) or IRA money invested in an index fund. So if you're early in your career, that may be a great option for you.

ENTREPRENEURSHIP

Investing is a wonderful option for making your money work for you because it's a mostly passive endeavor. If you're in the stock market, you make a deposit once or twice a month in a particular security, you leave it alone for several years, and you reap the benefits later (assuming good market conditions).

But if you're looking for something a little more challenging and potentially more rewarding, consider starting a business. It's going to require some elbow grease (a lot of it actually), particularly at the beginning when you are getting everything up and running. It won't be easy. And it'll take patience and persistence. But the beautiful thing about owning your own company is that you control your destiny. There is no boss or CEO running the show who may decide to cut your department one day. You are that CEO, and not only do you have control over your day-to-day, you also have the opportunity to create lasting wealth.

There are countless books you can read and podcasts you can listen to about the ins and outs of starting a business. So rather than try to go into specifics here, let's focus instead on some small business ideas you could get going, even while still working for someone else. If it grows into something bigger that could eventually replace that day job, great! You'll have even more control over your financial freedom when that day comes.

THE SIDE HUSTLE

Do you have a special talent or passion that you're not getting to exercise at your day job? Did you go to school for something different than what you do at work? Do your friends and family constantly ask you for your help with something in particular?

Then you may want to consider a side hustle. What is a side hustle, exactly? All it means is that you're doing something outside of your day job to help generate income. This can be anything from an online business that offers training to aspiring songwriters to selling handmade pottery on an Etsy shop. This can also be running a successful blog.

Whatever it is, most successful side hustles start of with the thought, *Gee, I wish I could do [insert an activity you like] for a living*. It can be liberating to realize that you don't have to do that activity full-time in order to do it at all.

You can start small. Baby step, after baby step. One day, you'll look back and be amazed by how far you've come.

Let's go back to the pottery example. If you're already making a few pieces a week because you love it, consider putting the completed pieces aside to try to sell. Look up Christmas markets or art festivals. Consider sharing your pieces on social media with prices. You may not make a ton of money right away. But you know what? If you make enough money to cover your expenses, then you're doing exactly what Robert Kiyosaki advises. You're finding other ways, outside your hard-earned paycheck, to fund your hobbies and interests.

Side hustles can also be a great way to save toward a bigger goal. If you're saving up for a down payment on a house and feel like it will take years at your current pace, you could put all the money you earn from freelance graphic design work into your savings account. You don't always have to strive toward your side hustle becoming your career. Instead, you can apply those skills toward achieving certain financial goals. By doing so, you take the progress toward that goal into your own hands.

PASSIVE INCOME

Passive income is exactly what it sounds like: It's money you make without actively working on it full-time, and it goes hand-in-hand with creating a side hustle.

Most often, side hustles outside of real estate are service based. You charge someone for a certain number of freelance hours, whether that means coaching leaders on their performance, teaching piano lessons, hosting a calligraphy workshop, or doing someone's taxes. In these cases, you're often trading time for money.

For most passive income streams, you invest some time on the front-end to develop a product that will require little work from you later when it sells. Think about online courses. Most often, there's no live instructor giving specialized lessons. Rather, you're likely to find prerecorded videos that will walk you through documents and exercises. And some of those courses work great! But guess what? When you enrolled in that class, the instructor very well may have been on their couch, watching TV.

The same goes for most fashion bloggers. Yes, they're doing work ahead of time by putting together outfits and getting photographed wearing them, but when readers click on links to go buy those clothing pieces, the blogger earns a commission. Those affiliate links, along with brand partnerships, provide a nice opportunity for a blogger to recoup the costs of their clothing. And for some hyper-successful bloggers, affiliate links alone can bring in big bucks going way beyond the cost of clothes.

Books, e-books, and online resources can also fall in this category. If you have a lot of knowledge about a topic, don't feel like you need to give it all away for free. Find a way to capture your knowledge so that other people can benefit from it without you needing to charge for one-on-one coaching hours.

The tough thing about establishing a passive income stream is that it often requires that people know who you are. So whether you build a reputation for yourself freelancing or build an online following over several months, getting your name out there in connection to your offering is key. And remember, every pro was once an amateur.

REAL ESTATE

As we wrap up talking about other ways to generate income, I'd be remiss if I didn't mention real estate. If investing and online products require very little up-front investment, real estate can require a bit more than that.

But if that side hustle is cruising along and you've found yourself with a healthy savings account, real estate should be your next big move.

When I talk about real estate, I don't just mean purchasing a house for yourself to live in. Rather, I mean purchasing a house or apartment complex for someone else to live in. When you have renters, their monthly rent should cover the costs of the mortgage and other expenses plus a little extra. After that initial investment, you'll essentially just collect checks from your renters every month. Talk about passive income!

Now, of course there will be plumbing problems and renovations to contend with. But if you're handy, you can tackle some of those things yourself. And as long as you keep a contingency fund for your properties, you'll be able to hire someone to help when the need arises.

In my case, my dad recommended buying a rental property before buying a house of my own. He told me to let the income I made from renters pay for my own down payment down the road. And that's exactly what I've done. By going this route of owning rental properties, it's created a flow of passive income outside of my "day job."

I understand that this may seem unattainable to some right now. But the more you begin to focus on putting your money to work for you, the more quickly you'll see it pay off. And after that, it begins to snowball. So keep this idea in the back of your mind for when the time is right.

FINDING YOUR PROFESSIONAL PATH

We've gone through a lot of different options for how to make sure you've found the right day job and how to bring in additional revenue. I hope that, at this point, you feel like the opportunities are endless. Because they are.

How then do you decide the right path for *you*?

The first thing to remember is that, like everything we've talked about so far, your professional life is yours. Pay no attention to the high-powered job your brother has or your friend's killer Instagram following. Keep your focus, first and foremost, on you and what you value.

Money is a super tough topic because we don't talk about it often with each other. So just keep in mind that while someone else may appear to be rocking it professionally, you really have no idea how they're doing financially.

So the best thing you can do is ignore all the noise, focus on yourself, and make sure that you're creating a sustainable path forward. In other words, you need to find things that fill you up, that fund the life you want, and that play to your strengths—while living within your means. With a mixture of initiatives that check off those boxes, you'll be on your way to financial freedom—without burning out after a few months.

So as you evaluate any new venture, start by asking yourself these four questions. If you're considering a freelancing side hustle, for example, you may not answer yes to every question. But if you answer no to all of them, walk away from that opportunity and look for something else.

So what are these questions? They're this:

▸ Will I enjoy this?

▸ Will this help me reach my financial goals?

▸ Am I good at this?

▸ Will this make a positive impact on those around me?

Let's dig into each of these questions a little more.

WILL I ENJOY THIS?

Let's just start with the easiest. Are you considering this venture solely because it will bring you money? Or are you hoping to fulfill a personal passion? Maybe you're somewhere in between and you kind of, sort of like it.

There's no right answer, but be sure to go into these kinds of decisions with eyes wide open. If you don't like what you're doing, there's a real chance you'll get bored of it pretty quickly. Or frustrated. Or angry. For example, if you absolutely hate talking on the phone, one-on-one coaching may not be your thing. You may dread those calls, which will cause you to dread the prep work that goes into them. Six months later, you may think, *Why did I even bother in the first place? This isn't worth the trouble.*

Doing something you hate isn't sustainable.

But if that coaching will help launch you toward a passive income product down the line, maybe it's worth sucking it up for a few months.

Who knows? Only you can know what you can tolerate, and sometimes you won't really know until you try.

I can guarantee you won't like every aspect of any job. If you run a creative business, you may really hate the accounting work that goes with it. But does the positive outweigh the negative?

And beyond that, do you have other positive areas of your professional life? Do you work for a nonprofit that fills you up every day, making those coaching calls easier?

WILL THIS HELP ME REACH MY FINANCIAL GOALS?

The next question to ask yourself is how much you stand to gain from an opportunity. This is where research and planning come into play. In short, don't let intuition drive your decision-making.

Take a look at the industry. How much will it cost you to get involved? If you want to launch an online course, what kind of fees will you pay? If you're looking at buying a rental property, how much are properties in the area going for? What's the split between renters and owners in that neighborhood?

Pay attention also to what competitors are charging. How will you price your product or service? Will that be enough to cover those expenses? How many customers would you need to break even?

It can be tempting when you have a good idea to want to jump in headfirst, but I encourage you to slow down. Do your homework first, and you'll feel much more confident in your decision when you do take your first step toward it.

If you're starting a new business, spend the needed time to draft a business plan. You may not be presenting it to investors, but filling in the key areas of a standard business plan will help you think through some pivotal questions about how you'll make money, when you'll make it, and what you need to do to spread the word about your company.

Once you've gathered all that information, spend some time getting honest with yourself about whether the potential payoff will be enough to justify the work you'll put in. This way of thinking also applies when considering accepting a traditional job. Will that paycheck make up for the aspects of the job you don't like? If so, great! Sign on the dotted line and accept the offer.

But if there's one thing I hope you get from this chapter, it's that there are several ways to make money. My hope is that you won't need to make tremendous sacrifices in your values or passions in the name of earning a paycheck.

AM I GOOD AT THIS?

This is a question that gets skipped over sometimes in books, articles, or podcasts about career planning and entrepreneurship. The thinking behind that is that we can learn to be good at anything if we try hard at it. But, if we're being honest, skill is important.

It's when we don't talk about skill that we end up with situations like the blogger who doesn't understand why her web traffic hasn't grown or the consultant who can't seem to get referrals. If someone is going to pay you for something, they need to know that you're an expert in that area. Or, at the very least, more of an expert than they are.

So before you go down the road of coming up with a business idea that has nothing to do with your past experience, spend some time examining your current skill set. What are you already good at? What do your friends come to you for advice on? Can you monetize that, instead?

By doing so, you'll be heading off years of study and practice.

This applies especially to those just starting off. I didn't know much about what a real estate agent did when I decided to go after my agent's license. But I did have a few other streams of income going at the time, so I had the flexibility to learn while keeping those streams going.

WILL THIS HAVE A POSITIVE IMPACT ON THOSE AROUND ME?

Last but not least, spend some time analyzing your potential for impact and whether having a large impact is important to you. When it comes to having a positive impact, we often think of people who are out there saving the world, taking in very little for themselves.

The truth is that there are many ways to measure impact. Maybe you're looking to solve a common problem for a group of people or provide a new product or service that will make life easier on some people. Maybe your company donates to charity or only works with socially responsible vendors.

There are many, many ways to have a positive impact, whether on a small group of people or the world at large. I encourage you to consider your potential for positive impact alongside the other criteria mentioned previously, like financial stability and personal skills, because there is no greater reward than helping others in some way.

Now, let's spend a few minutes brainstorming ideas together, and let's start with your personal skills. **What are some of your unique abilities? In what circumstances do people ask you for advice? Spend at least 5 minutes thinking about it, and write down what comes to mind.**

You're off to a great start!

Now, write down the things that you love doing. What are your hobbies? What do you like about your job (or what did you like about past jobs)? Which activities fill you with energy?

....

....

....

Are you seeing any overlap? Is there anything you love doing that you happen to be good at, too?

Let's bring it all together now by looking at what you've written down. **What could you do to monetize what you wrote down? Are there opportunities to teach those skills to others, to write about it, to speak or podcast about it? Don't block yourself from writing down any idea. Just freewrite what comes to mind!**

....

....

....

....

And last but not least, consider your potential for positive impact. **How could this idea positively help or support others? What could you do to create good?**

_____

_____

_____

_____

If a clear picture of a perfect side hustle or dream job didn't appear, don't worry. If it were easy, everyone would do it. Use this as a jumping off point and keep thinking about these three questions as new ideas come to you.

And remember: Do your homework before jumping in to anything.

DON'T FORGET!

Before we wrap up this chapter, there are a few other ideas worth touching on. I mentioned earlier that doing things you hate just isn't sustainable. But guess what? Doing something you love may not be sustainable either if you put too much on your plate. So we'll switch gears briefly to talk about *how* to implement these new ideas—and how to do so without burning out.

YOUR OTHER PILLARS

Do you remember all the way back in the Physical Pillar chapter when we talked about how being physically active can actually make you more productive?

And in the Emotional Pillar, when we talked about how emotional strength can help you deal with challenging situations, at work or at home?

And even in the Mental Pillar, when we talked about mental curiosity helping to expand your horizons?

I bring all of these examples up to remind you of the interconnectedness of the Pillars. Each one has an impact on the other, and when one is ignored or left by the wayside, a domino effect can ensue. If you focus all of your attention on your professional goals and ignore your physical fitness, for example, you may find that you have less energy. Maybe you're less focused. Maybe even your health starts to suffer.

And if any of those things happen, you're not really getting closer to your professional goals, are you? If you are, you won't be able to keep up that pace forever.

But if you give each Pillar some attention, even just a little bit, you'll be amazed at what you can achieve. Our society idealizes the hustle. We love to talk about the entrepreneurs who wake up before dawn and the side hustlers making their dreams come true by working late into the night. I am a total advocate for going after your dreams, but I am a bigger advocate for making sure that you don't lose yourself, your health, or your relationships in the process.

Remember: The goal is to be better than you were yesterday—not just in one Pillar but in all of them.

Because if your primary goals lie in the Professional Pillar, the others are going to help you achieve them. Each Pillar, when given some attention, can have tremendous positive effects on the others.

So the next time you feel unfocused or down, go on a walk. When you feel like you don't have any good ideas, read a book or talk to someone you don't know well. When you feel sad or upset, read a passage from the Bible or go to a church service. Allow your community to pick you back up. And when you set lofty goals to achieve financial freedom, don't lose sight of why you want to achieve it in the first place.

EMBRACE MENTORSHIP

We started the chapter talking about mentors, and we'll end there, too. I said before that it's unlikely you'll have just one mentor in your professional life, someone who can answer all your questions about career advancement, entrepreneurship, investing, and more.

But just because it's unlikely to find a single guru, that doesn't mean mentorship should be passed over. Sure you can do research and learn everything you want about the stock market, but wouldn't it be so much faster to pick the brain of someone who has been investing successfully already?

There is no need to reinvent the wheel when you don't need to. Mentors help us cut to the chase and supply us with information we need to know much faster than if we were to go out and research everything ourselves.

And when you have more than one mentor you can lean on, you can compare and contrast their ideas. A friend of mine, for example, recently started doing some freelance coaching in the evenings after work. As he was getting his business up and running, he reached out to three or four people he knew who were doing similar work, and he asked them all the same question: How were the majority of their clients finding them?

One person immediately mentioned her newsletter and talked about the importance of a strong website with incentives to get people to join the newsletter list.

Another said that almost 100% of his business came through word of mouth. He attended a lot of networking events and treated every info call, no matter how unqualified the lead was, with the highest level of care and respect.

Another talked about attending industry events and conferences. He was there to learn new skills, sure, but he found that building relationships at these events and making friendships ultimately led to referrals and business.

So you see, there are no right answers. Other people can achieve the same goals you set for yourself by doing vastly different things. What worked for them may not work for you, so it's worth finding a few reliable mentors to bounce ideas off of, ask questions, and find out what works for you.

And now I'm going to share some of the best advice I've learned through having many mentors over the years: When you're ready to ask for help, be thoughtful with your questions and keep your ask focused and deliberate.

Share a challenge you're facing or a situation or opportunity you'd welcome perspective on. Think of one or two questions that you just can't figure out on your own, at least without hours of research. The narrower your focus, the more valuable your conversation will be. Rather than broad advice that may or may not apply to you, you'll leave with actionable steps you can try out.

You will also show your mentors that you respect their time. They're not there to solve every problem for you or to walk you through how to run a business, step-by-step. They're there to help you with what you need most and sometimes to share insights into things you may not even know you need yet.

But mentors will not just fall into your lap. Put yourself out there through events, classes, webinars, and networking. Look for people who have done what you'd like to do or something similar. Build a relationship with them, and then ask for their guidance. The mentor relationship starts with *you*. If you don't seek out the people you admire and cultivate the relationship, you'll miss out on some incredibly valuable experiences. And this should happen naturally. Don't force it. If it pans out, the feeling will be mutual.

More than anything, know that you are not alone in your quest to be better than you were yesterday. There are many, many people out there with all the expertise and compassion to help you along your path. You just have to find them. And you have to ask.

And with that, we've wrapped up our last Pillar. We have covered so much ground, and I hope you're proud of the amount of work you have already put into improving your life.

Next comes the fun part. The next chapter is where we'll put it all together. We'll take a deep dive into our own personal values, we'll figure out which Pillars are most important to us, and we'll set some goals. More than anything, you're going to create your own game plan for what to do when you've finished the book. The work doesn't stop when you turn the last page, and I'm not sending you off without a boost.

Let's do some soul searching.

CHAPTER 8

WHAT DO YOU STAND FOR?

"Outstanding people have one thing in common:
An absolute sense of mission."

–ZIG ZIGLAR

TWENTY-FOUR HOURS. That's how much time we have in a day. It sounds like a lot, right? If we could focus for twenty-four hours straight, imagine how much we could get done. Starting a side hustle would be a piece of cake. We'd never skip a workout. The house would always be spotless.

But that's not exactly realistic, is it? Instead, there are so many things that we have to do in a day that can get in the way of the things we want to do. Let's do some quick math.

Sleep should take up about eight of those hours, leaving us with only sixteen waking hours left.

Then there's work. Let's say you work in a steady nine-to-five environment. That's another eight, and if the average commute is half an hour each way, add one more. Now we're down to only seven hours left for us and things we want to do.

We have to eat, right? Subtract an hour for dinner, and now we're down to six hours.

What about your morning routine? Let's assume an hour for showering, getting ready, enjoying a cup of coffee, and whatever else you do to wake yourself up for the day. Five hours left.

Then there are the things we don't do everyday but that inevitably get in the way of enjoying five hours of whatever we want to do. Maybe it's a trip to the grocery store, an oil change, a load of laundry, picking up the kids from soccer practice, or running to the dry cleaners.

When all is said and done, there are usually only a few short hours left at the end of the day for choice. Do you spend that time working out? Watching TV? Doing some freelance work? Meeting friends for happy hour? Maybe you try to do a little bit of everything (and I'm guessing that doesn't go as well as you'd like).

It begins to feel like time is slipping through our fingers.

This is why understanding your personal values is so profoundly important. We have so many choices to make surrounding how we spend our time, but we have very little actual time if we don't take charge of it. We can't do everything we want in just a few hours a day. And the more goals we set for ourselves, the more valuable those hours become.

In other words, our values determine our goals, and our goals determine how we spend our time.

As you've been reading, I hope that you've been giving each Pillar equal billing—that you've focused intently on the Pillar at hand and embraced the daily exercises that accompany each one.

While all of the Pillars are important to a strong foundation, the truth is that they are not created equal. Depending on who you are and what you value, some Pillars will be more important to you than others. By spending time and concentrating deeply on each Pillar, you hopefully now have a clear understanding of how they rank for you.

Maybe you felt energized and driven while reading the Mental

Pillar, but the Professional Pillar weighed you down. Or maybe the Spiritual Pillar spoke to you, while the Physical Pillar was less interesting. Which challenges did you look forward to most? Which were you less excited about?

It's my belief that ignoring any one Pillar altogether would leave you with some pretty negative consequences. But by understanding the order of their importance to you, you'll avoid tearing your hair out from trying to do it all at once.

Our goal is to be better than we were yesterday. That doesn't necessarily mean you take one step forward in each Pillar every day. Some days, you may take three steps forward professionally and one step forward in a few other Pillars. Other days, you'll take one step forward Spiritually and Physically, and that's it.

In other words, it is tough to progress in each area of our lives at the same pace. We have to decide what matters most to us.

So let's start there. On our way to figuring out our personal values, let's evaluate how the Pillars rank for you. Next to each Pillar below, rank them 1–5, 1 being the most important to you and 5 being the least.

_____ Physical

_____ Mental

_____ Emotional

_____ Spiritual

_____ Professional

How did that feel?

Hopefully you felt some relief! We're all guilty of putting too much pressure on ourselves to do it all. Did it feel nice to give yourself a little grace and admit that you don't need progress in each Pillar at the same pace?

As we move through the rest of this chapter and hone in on your personal values and mission statement, my hope is that you'll begin to feel more and more weight removed from your shoulders. The more you understand what *you* value and what goals *you* want to achieve, along with the *why* behind them, things will begin to click into place. You'll become more sure of how to spend your valuable time. You'll start achieving your personal goals. And bit by bit, you'll be on your way to a fulfilled life.

The process of becoming your best self should be an energizing, exciting experience! For that reason, I encourage you to take advantage of the writing space provided. The more you engage with the exercises, the more real your progress will become and the more you will commit to following through on your goals.

SETTING THE RIGHT FRAME OF MIND

Before we jump into defining your values, let's start by getting into the right mindset. In the Mental Pillar, we talked about the importance of cultivating gratitude and the effect that it can have on our mindset.

Gratitude can help us find the stillness we need to evaluate our lives. It can help us put our problems and worries into perspective. It can also put us in a better mood, plain and simple. We should always start new things from a stance of gratitude. Heck, we should start each day with gratitude. So let's put that idea into practice, shall we?

I'd like to start off by cultivating gratitude about your life journey so far through three different gratitude exercises. In each, spend some time going back through the archives of your memory. Think about the events and people that had profoundly positive impacts on you. Whether they were small or large, allow yourself to be grateful for them and the role they played in your life.

GRATITUDE EXERCISE #1

Write down a time when you felt unquestionably happy. What comes to mind first? Which memory keeps coming back up as you think of other times? What were you doing? Who were you with? What about the experience made you happy?

Freewrite about this experience and try to capture as many details as possible.

_____

_____

_____

_____

GRATITUDE EXERCISE #2

Write down your three proudest moments. Think back through your memories and try to remember times when you were most proud of yourself. What were the circumstances around that event? What sparked your sense of pride? Who else was involved in that memory?

Write down whatever comes to mind for each memory.

1. _____

_____

_____

2. _____

_____

_____

3. _____

_____

_____

GRATITUDE EXERCISE #3

Now we're going to have some fun. Grab yourself a cup of coffee. Make yourself comfortable. Settle in for at least 15 to 20 minutes if you're able, and commit to this exercise.

Write down the 10 things you feel most grateful for you in your life. They don't need to be specific memories or people. It can be as simple as writing the word "health." They don't need to be ranked in order, but be thoughtful about your responses. Ask yourself if each item you write down truly belongs among the things you are *most* grateful for in life.

Once you have your 10 things, write them here.

1. _____

2. _____

3. _____

4. _____

5. _____

6. _____

7. _____

8. ....

9. ....

10. ....

How are you feeling? High on life and like you can conquer anything? Good!

It can feel strange to let yourself revel in the good in your life, almost like if we pay too much attention to the good, something terrible will happen. Well, I'm here to tell you that there's no point thinking that way. In fact, practicing gratitude not only helps us gain perspective on the negative things that do come our way but it also helps us to get a clear picture of what matters most to us.

Are you most grateful for your family or friends? Do you absolutely love your morning walks? Identifying what fills you with a deep sense of gratitude is the first step toward identifying your values. After all, if you don't recognize what fills you up, how can you intentionally cultivate more of it in your life?

So let these positive emotions stay with you as you complete this chapter. Review your answers if you start to feel overwhelmed or down on yourself. Before each exercise that remains, check in and ask if you are starting in a place of gratitude.

YOUR INNER CIRCLE

It's pretty easy to feel gratitude for relationships. When you're part of a strong, positive, and motivating relationship of any kind, you just feel good. Hopefully there are a few people that you care deeply for and that you consider yourself lucky to have in your life. Building connection with other people brings a sense of community and support, and it allows for enormous personal growth. We all have our strengths, and when we get together, those strengths begin to rub off on each other. Iron sharpens iron, remember?

Consider who in your life makes you feel smarter. Who gets you to open up and talk about your feelings? Who do you trust to share your spiritual questions with?

I mentioned relationships in every single Pillar because they are vital to self-improvement, no matter how you're aiming to improve. When you surround yourself with people who lift you up, you will find the journey toward becoming your best self will be a lot easier and a lot more fun. Besides, when there are so many incredible people in the world, why go it alone or with people who will pull you back? So let's take a look at the people surrounding you currently and the effect they have over you.

RELATIONSHIPS EXERCISE #1

Who do you interact with most in your life? Write down their name, and, beside it, write down the Pillar(s) that they most align with. The people closest to you likely lift you up in multiple categories. That said, if you're struggling to see how someone improves your life, leave it blank.

NAME   **PILLAR(S)**

_____

_____

_____

_____

RELATIONSHIPS EXERCISE #2

Did you notice any patterns in the last exercise? Do you have lots of spiritual friends from your Bible study group but no one to exercise with? We all have these kinds of gaps, and there's no right answer for how many relationships you should have. Some of us need a lot of social interaction, while others just need a few close connections. But if you've noticed that any Pillars are absent from your list above, begin to explore your secondary connections.

Write down a list of people that you would like to spend more time with to help fill in those gaps. If no one springs to mind, that's okay! It's always possible to make new friends. But start by acknowledging it here in general terms. It can be as simple as writing down, "I'd like a buddy to hike with on weekends."

RELATIONSHIP EXERCISE #3

Hopefully the last two exercises have gotten you thinking about the roles that the people in your life play in your development. If you've noticed that some people just don't line up with your values anymore, that's okay. But let's end on a more positive note. Write down the three people you most admire and why. Pay attention to what it is you admire about them.

1. _____

2. _____

3. _____

RELATIONSHIP EXERCISE #4

Relationships are a two-way street. In order to deepen the ones you care most about, some introspection about what you bring to the table will be helpful. So be honest with yourself and write down the ways in which you sharpen others? What do your friends value *you* for?

_____

_____

_____

_____

In an ideal world, we'd all walk through life with friends, family members, and partners who always lift us up and never let us down. While it's important to seek out relationships with people who can strengthen you in certain areas of your life, it's also worth recognizing the complexities of people. You will not be a perfect friend, and neither will they.

There's no use in cutting someone out of your life because they mess up a few times. But if negative experiences become habitual, there's also no use in hanging on to a toxic relationship that doesn't serve you or your goals. You only get one life. Try to spend it with people who also recognize that fact and will help you make the most of it.

YOUR PRECIOUS SPARE TIME

The next step toward identifying our values goes back to time. Where are those precious few hours going at the end of the day? As we talked about earlier, it can easily feel like we have no control over them, but by bringing awareness to and writing down the things we enjoy doing and want to do more of, we'll start to regain some control.

Hopefully, we'll begin to prioritize the things that matter most and set some goals around them. And at the very least, this added awareness will help us start to recognize patterns of the kinds of things that get in the way.

Let's start with an inventory of how you've been spending your time. Then we'll have some fun and talk about how you *want* to spend it.

TIME EXERCISE #1

Write down your current hobbies and activities. When all the items on the "have-to-do" list are done, what do you do? Consider fitness, mental stimulation, spirituality, and anything else that you do for you.

TIME EXERCISE #2

Write down the activities you wish you had more time for. What would you like to spend your time doing?

TIME EXERCISE #3

Now, I'd like for you to write down the things you have an interest in but have never tried. What are some things you're curious about? What sounds really fun? Even if it's something off the wall and out of character, like horseback riding or computer coding, write it down! I won't force you to do it, but allow yourself to open up and be honest about your potential interests. Get as far away from the "have-to-do" list as you can.

Look at all that you've already written down about yourself and the people in your life. You've done quite the personal inventory and should be hugely proud of the emotional work you've put in to complete these exercises with total honesty.

Real honesty can make you feel vulnerable, but it can also make you feel powerful. You know what you care most about, who you care most about, and how to make time in your life for them. Do you feel more in control of your destiny now? Do you feel like you know yourself better and that happiness is in your grasp?

Excellent! Because it is in your grasp. We're about to put all of the previous exercises together into something more succinct: your values.

YOUR VALUES

All of the work you've done so far in the book has been done in order to help you discover what you really care about most in life. You focused intently on one Pillar at a time so that you wouldn't write any of them off or spend too much time on any one. It was an opportunity to play, to experiment, and to try new things. Maybe it reaffirmed what you already thought about yourself, or maybe you learned something new and surprising.

Whatever the work you've done so far has shown you about yourself, you are ready. With a better understanding of who you are, who you spend time with, and what you care about, you know what your values are. You just need to dedicate time to thinking them through and writing them down.

For perspective, I'll give you some of mine: relationships, optimism, go-getting, ethics, honesty, trust, perseverance, poise, growth, peace, fun, and faith. They are the words that describe who I am and are lived out in my actions every day.

Your values are the basis of your character and should stand the test of time. Even as you grow and change, your values will remain the same. They are the essence of who you are and who you will become. So in evaluating your values, you are answering the questions: What do you believe? Who do you believe you are?

On top of that, they dictate how others view you, the question becoming: Does who you think you are line up with how other people view you? If you want to be known as honest and a true friend, would other people agree with that? If not, there's a disconnect that needs to be sorted out. Do you really value friendship as much as you think? If so, how do your daily actions demonstrate that value to the people around you?

As you consider your values, think about both sides of the coin: what you believe and how others view you. What do those perceptions tell you about your values? If there's a disconnect, what do they tell you about who you want to become?

A final word of advice: Don't overanalyze this exercise at first. Values are important to identify, but the process of doing so likely won't be as challenging as you initially think. Look back through your answers to the previous exercises. Think about the things you do with your time and who you do them with. What are the biggest sources of joy for you? You'll start to see some patterns. Maybe the word "family" keeps appearing. Maybe your relationships and activities center around gaining knowledge. Allow your values to be as specific or broad as they need to be. Then walk away from the exercise for a few minutes, read your list, and decide if they all feel right. More than anything, this is an exercise in allowing yourself to feel intently and listen to your gut.

Write down your top 3–5 values here.

YOUR PERSONAL MISSION STATEMENT

Way back in the first chapter, I shared my personal mission statement with you. It reads:

To live a faith-driven life focused on finding the good things in life and positively impacting those around me.

Looking at that statement, you can probably figure out a few of my values, can't you? Faith, optimism, impact, and relationships. These are huge for me, and combining them into one statement gives me a succinct mantra to remember everyday.

It's a litmus test to ask, *Am I living in accordance with my values?* If

I'm following my mission statement, then you can bet I am. And when I'm faced with a tough, intimidating decision, rereading my own mission statement usually points me in the right direction.

All too often, people ignore the concept of having a personal mission statement. They may think it's not for them or that it's only for companies. It's actually quite the opposite. Just like companies have a mission statement to guide their firm, you too should have one to guide your life. It keeps you on track, keeps you focused, and keeps you grounded.

You've done the hard work already by identifying your values. Now is the time to start thinking about the actions you'll take to live them. What will you stand for? How will you behave toward others?

A personal mission statement should be timeless, without language of goals or dreams. You should be able to check if you are living in accordance with it every single day. Because, while there may be some days when you don't see noticeable progress in your goals, if you've lived that day in line with your mission, you've still succeeded in growing. The more your mission statement becomes a part of you, the ultimate habit, the easier it becomes to live out your values. So every day that you live in accordance with it, you have taken steps toward strengthening that habit.

Take as much time as you need. When you're ready, write down your mission statement. Tell me what you stand for.

Reading it back, how do you feel about that statement? Proud, I hope! If someone were to ask you what you stand for, you should be able to vocalize your personal mission with confidence because, if you've done it with complete honesty and vulnerability, you know that it is a real, accurate representation of you. And that is something to shout from the rooftops.

Keep your mission statement close to you, either written down somewhere you see everyday or repeated in your mind each day. Keeping it front and center will help to ensure that you stand strong in your mission and that you don't get sucked into living someone else's. Be aware that other people will be living out their own missions and acknowledge that that's perfectly okay. You don't need to adopt theirs, and they don't need to explicitly adopt yours. We're all on our own journeys here, and we can support each other along our individual paths through respect and appreciation for our differences.

GOOOOAAAAAAAAAALS!

With our mission statements completed, we're starting to gain some momentum around living our values. There's action. There's movement. There's amazing progress being done just by living in accordance with them. But what about the other things we want to accomplish—the big things?

Well, those kinds of dreams require a little more planning. They require that we set goals and work steadily and intentionally to achieve them. In other words, rather than waiting for decisions to pop up and responding according to our values, goals allow us to take things into our own hands. They enable us to go out into the world and do the things that will bring us long-term fulfillment.

Not only that, goals are amazing benchmarks for showing us just how far we've come. I remember a brutal training run a few months before running the New York City Marathon when I questioned if I'd be able to do it. Based on how exhausted I was running 15 miles, 26.2 seemed so far out of reach. And when I crossed the finish line of the marathon, I remembered that moment of apprehension. It made completing the race even more sweet. I worked hard for it, and I changed in so many ways as a result of pushing myself to accomplish that goal.

To set and reach your own goals, there are three simple steps to follow:

1 **IDENTIFY WHERE YOU WANT TO BE.** What is the result of the goal? What effect will reaching it have on you?

2 **IDENTIFY THE STEPS YOU NEED TO TAKE TO GET THERE.** Get granular. Make a schedule. Figure out exactly how much work you'll need to do to accomplish your goal, working backward from your answer to #1 to where you are now.

3 **MAKE IT SMART.** Double check that your goal is specific, measurable, achievable, relevant, and time-oriented.

Your goals can involve anything you want, but if you're stuck, I recommend starting small. What's something you can accomplish in a week or a month? With every small goal you check off your list, you'll be practicing the three steps above and you'll be proving to yourself that you can do it. That way, when a big goal like starting a freelance business or reading 20 books a year comes along, you'll have the confidence and skill to know you can handle it. In other words, you may also want to run a marathon one day. But before you can do that, you have to be able to run a mile.

Let's start out by writing down five simple, meaningful goals that you can accomplish in a short time frame. Unless you have a few that you're itching to start, try to select one goal from each Pillar. And don't forget to think through the steps you'll need to take and to make them SMART.

1. ....

....

2. ....

....

3. ....

....

4. ....

....

5. ....

....

Great! So how do we make sure these goals don't go the way of our January diet plans of years past? In other words, how do we make sure we complete these goals? There are many ways to hold yourself accountable. It starts, first and foremost, with will. You have to *want* to achieve the goal. And to go even deeper, you must understand "why" you want to achieve that goal. If you're *why* is strong enough, everything else will fall into place

Since the goals you wrote down above were thought up with your values and mission statement in mind, I'm going to bet you care about them a great deal. So if you start to question why you want these goals, go back to your values and your mission. Remember that you are on a continuous journey toward self-improvement and that these goals will help you live the life you've been dreaming of. In moments of doubt and uncertainty, focus on your mindset. How can you get back to the state of mind you were in when you wrote down your goals?

SET YOURSELF UP FOR SUCCESS

We've talked at length already about the power of gratitude to change your mindset, but it bears repeating here. Start a daily gratitude practice. Write down things you are grateful for every evening before bed. Doing so will help to keep you in the right frame of mind to achieve your goals, rather than spiraling down into negative emotions.

Surround yourself with positive motivation. Are there quotes that motivate you? What about songs that get you pumped up and feeling happy? What about a funny desktop background or serene painting on your wall? Do you feel better in a brightly lit room with natural light? Do you always feel inspired after coming home from a short walk? Do you feel energized after spending time around certain people?

Pay attention to the external triggers that spark enthusiasm and engagement, and make an active choice to surround yourself with those things. If walks always get you going, don't roll out of bed and head straight to your computer. Make time for the things that will make you more productive and happy.

Likewise, get rid of the negative influences. If the news zaps you of all your enthusiasm, catch up on it later in the day. If your gym makes you feel intimidated and insecure, try a different, more welcoming one. And cultivate your circle of friends, family, and mentors to surround yourself with. Pay no attention to the people who leave you feeling down.

When you're in the right frame of mind, there is little you can't do. You can achieve all those goals on your list—I know it's possible! But if you let the negative influences start to invade, you'll lose steam. When you pay attention to where your energy goes and what drives it away, you can start to take control over your mindset and, as a result, your productivity.

On top of changing your mindset, we are also going to work on making goal setting (and goal achievement) a habit. All along, that is what the daily challenges have been intended to do. Each day, you have been checking off a small goal. We're going to keep going with these daily challenges, but now you're going to write your own daily challenges, customized to who you are and what you value.

30 DAYS OF CHANGE

The daily challenges have been an exercise in branching out and exploring what's possible. I hope that you discovered some new things that you enjoyed, and I hope that you pushed yourself just a tiny bit harder to becoming the person you want to be. I'm sure some of the challenges felt downright silly, while others just felt *right*. (Just know that the ones that felt silly for you felt just right for others.)

One of the cool things about doing challenges concentrating around one Pillar at a time is that you probably also got to see some growth. Maybe after parking a little farther away at the grocery store and doing some extra push-ups in the morning, you felt more energy. You were able to feel the side effects of your combined challenges.

When we talk about goal setting, we're talking about the same basic concept. One of the key steps in completing a goal is breaking down the steps you need to take to get there. If your goal was to feel healthier, parking a little farther away and doing some push-ups in the morning may have been those steps for you.

The daily challenges, more than anything, were meant to start forming a habit within you to think about your goals every day. Now that you have an idea of which Pillars are most important to you and what your overall values are, it's time for you to take the reins. You'll start by breaking down those goals you wrote down earlier into smaller and smaller activities. Just remember, it starts with baby steps.

What are things you can do to work toward those goals that can be accomplished in a single day?

At the end of this book, you'll find a blank calendar. Fill in the calendar with your own daily challenges that will help you to achieve those goals. If you want to apply to a new job, for example, you could assign one day to cleaning up your resume, one day to researching opportunities, and another day to writing your cover letter. See how the goal starts to feel more manageable when you break it into its component parts?

As you start to fill up your calendar with challenges, stop to consider balance. Are you covering all 5 Pillars? If one of the Pillars is noticeably absent, keep one or two days reserved for it. Remember that together, they form a strong foundation. If one is neglected and begins to crumble, that foundation weakens. (So by all means, don't trade sleep for any of the goals on your list.)

And if you're at a loss for how to fill some days, consult the list you made in Time Exercise #3. What are some things you're curious about but haven't tried? Push yourself to explore your interests even more. After all, this is a life-long journey you're on, and you won't know what your tastes are in all cases unless you give new things a try. Change and variety are great things, so continue to seek out new and different experiences.

It's not all about pushing and driving for more each and every day. It's also about having fun and enjoying life along the way. Do you remember way back in this book when we talked about scheduling our lives away? We schedule absolutely everything, from dentist appointments to play-dates for our kids. But we don't schedule fun. We don't schedule self-care. Now you've got a calendar where you can plan out exactly that, alongside the harder stuff like investing money or reading news articles. Trust me on this: You will not regret planning for fun.

And you know what else is pretty great? You are not in this alone.

THE ALWAYSSMILIN COMMUNITY

I've talked a lot about family so far in this book, and I'd like you to join mine now. The AlwaysSmilin community is a family, ready to support you on your path to happiness and fulfillment. They're your cheerleaders, your biggest fans, and your confidantes all rolled into one because they're on the same journey. They may not be taking the same path, but they're also hoping to end up with a sense of pure fulfillment.

So when you need the support, I encourage you to look to Always-Smilin for encouragement. The inspirational quotes will be there for you when you need them. Blog posts will help give you strategies to keep going. But more than that, the people of the community will rally around you to lift you up. All you have to do is talk to them and use the #AlwaySmilinProgress hashtag to connect.

When you engage with the community, you can be sure positive vibes will be coming your way. Show us photos of yourself achieving your goals or talk to us about what's holding you back. And when you see someone else who could use some encouragement, pay it forward. Reach out with kind words and enthusiasm. Be the spark that keeps someone else on track to reach their goals. A rising tide lifts all boats. We are in this together. We've got each others' backs.

And you are ready. You have accomplished so much already. Just think what you can do with the knowledge you've gained and the support you have behind you now. You can achieve the life you dream about, and you can be as happy and fulfilled as you've always hoped.

It's in your reach. You just have to begin at Day 1.

MOVING FORWARD & CREATING POSITIVE IMPACT

"In every day, there are 1,440 minutes. That means we have
1,440 daily opportunities to make a positive impact."

–LES BROWN

CROSSING THE FINISH LINE at the New York City Marathon years ago was a feeling unlike any I had experienced in my life so far. I was exhausted and elated, surprised at myself and full of confidence at the same time. Tiredness and joy mixed together in a way that left me breathless. Literally.

After months of training, countless early morning runs, healthy eating decisions, and more water than I thought was possible for one person to drink, I knew that all of the effort was worth it. I had accomplished a major goal of mine. I had worked and sweated for something that mattered, and at that moment when my feet crossed the finish line, I could tell without a doubt that I was the best version of myself so far. It was pure joy.

And then I looked over at Joslyn, who had finished well ahead of me, and that feeling doubled.

She absolutely beamed while also fighting back tears in her eyes. I could see that she was experiencing a wide range of emotions in that instant, and I felt honored to stand there by her side as volunteers slipped medals over our heads and we walked hand in hand toward our friends who had cheered us on.

To this day, this story is a powerful reminder for me of two important lessons. The first is to realize that accomplishing one goal almost always leads to another, that the work is never really done. And the second is that our goals, no matter how individualistic they may seem, connect us deeply to others.

After finishing 26.2 miles, the thought of running one more seemed impossible. I had pushed my body to its limits, and I looked forward to a few days without any physical activity whatsoever. I couldn't wait to go out to eat with friends, lay on the couch reading a book, or watch a movie with Jos. In the few days after the race, I was game for just about anything—except running.

When we complete big goals, it's easy to think, *Well, that was fun. I'm glad I never have to do that again.* We mentally cross that goal off the bucket list and move on to something else. There's a sense of finality.

I don't know if I'll ever run a marathon again, but I knew even then that I hadn't run my last mile ever. Without a doubt, I needed a break from it, but accomplishing this goal didn't mean giving up the hobby altogether. I knew that in a few weeks I'd be itching to go on a morning run.

Even if you're goal is to go skydiving to overcome your fear of heights, accomplishing that goal certainly means that you don't have to jump out of a plane again if you don't want. But occasionally you will need to go in a tall building or fly in a plane.

So as you embark on your own goals, remember that your goals should take you on a lifelong journey. Crossing things off your list for the sake of saying you've done it ultimately won't serve you. Push yourself to your limits, test your personal boundaries, and when you reach a goal, take the time to celebrate your accomplishment. You are stronger and more capable than you knew before. Allow that confidence to propel you to a new, even bigger goal.

The challenge of being better than you were the day before is in realizing that the work never stops. You may cross a finish line or jump out of a plane, but tomorrow you are tasked with making yourself even better in some way. Does that mean accomplishing a bigger feat? Not necessarily. What it does mean is shedding the natural inclination to think that when we accomplish a goal, we're done.

Every single day, we need to show up for ourselves. We need to put in the time and the effort to grow and improve. What that looks like each day will be entirely up to you. But when you've completed your 30 days of change, resist that feeling of finality and begin looking instead to your next 30 days, while remembering to have fun along the way.

Our lives are an enormous gift. We owe it to ourselves to make personal improvement a hobby and a lifelong goal. We owe it to ourselves to take full advantage of this gift every single day. We owe it to ourselves to decide what our own happiness and fulfillment look like and to go after it with everything we have. Every. Single. Day.

On top of that, we owe it to ourselves to find the people who will help us get there, the ones who propel us toward our goals instead of holding us back from them.

If you remember from the beginning of the book, the idea to run the marathon started with Jos as a way to honor her father. We ran in support of a charity that benefitted cancer research. On top of spending months training for the physical aspect of the run, we also raised money and shared information about the charity. There was emotional and mental work to be done in addition to the physical training.

When I looked at her after the race, I knew that we had accomplished something great together. I recognized that I may not have realized this goal without her asking me to sign up with her or pushing me through training runs.

I also knew that no medal they placed around my neck could ever stack up to the joy I felt in being there for her in return. Because, at the end of the day, while this goal meant a ton to both of this, it was a goal especially close to her heart.

In running the marathon, she didn't just take the steps needed to get her across the finish line. She honored a promise she had made to her father. She brought awareness and thousands of dollars to cancer research. And she took a big step forward in healing from his loss.

There isn't a doubt in my mind that Joslyn was also the best version of herself that she had been so far, and I will *never* forget being a part of that moment.

As you embark on your own journey, go into it clearheaded about what you want. Seek out the things that will bring you happiness and fulfillment. Seek out the people who will raise you up. As Thoreau said, "Live the life you've imagined."

And don't forget to raise others up in return.

More often than you may expect, you'll discover that helping someone you love achieve their own goals will support your happiness, rather than come into conflict with it. After all, the people you love are in your life for a reason, likely because you share the same values or passions. Look for ways to apply your own strengths and insights to help those around you.

Happiness is contagious. As you find your own happiness, be the spark that inspires others to discover theirs, too. Recognize that no two people will view happiness the same, but know that our own happiness is magnified when shared with others.

We walk through life hand in hand with other people. No one goes it alone. And when I think back to the marathon and to other major events in my own life, I am forever grateful. It's in these moments of shared experiences and shared emotions that we begin to understand the depths of our own happiness. We begin to see how fulfilled we can really be.

YOUR DAILY CHALLENGES

APPENDIX A

THE PHYSICAL PILLAR

PHYSICAL ACTIVITY

- Park farther away at the grocery store, gym, office, or work.

- When you wake up, do 10 push-ups immediately.

- Go for a morning jog. Put your shoes and clothes by your bed before going to sleep.

- Try a new sport or activity, like swimming, hiking, volleyball, etc. Just pick something you don't do often.

- Sign up for a gym membership (or a free trial!) and set a goal to go at least twice a week.

- Explore a new hobby that requires physical activity, like gardening.

- Do 10 body weight squats before your next shower.

- Ask a physically active friend to hang out. Go on a hike, walk your dogs together, or play a sport.

- Take a yoga class.

- Create a calendar event to work out later in the week. Make sure you stick to it.

- Sign up for a race, like a 5k or a 10k. Set a goal for yourself to complete it. If you've done one before, set a goal for your pace.

- Bring awareness to your posture today. When you catch yourself slouching, sit or stand up straight. Make a note for your desk if you need to!

- Schedule an annual physical with your doctor. You're never too young to start!

HEALTHY EATING

- Go a whole day without eating processed food. If you can't read the ingredient list, skip it.
- Drink at least 64 oz. of water today. Use a refillable water bottle and keep track of how much you've had.
- Skip alcohol for a weekend. Then try it for a week.
- Take time this evening to plan out your meals for the next 3 days. Go to the store and prepare all of your ingredients. Try to pick something healthy!
- Pick one unhealthy food that you love (and eat often) and give it up for 1 week.
- Cut out caffeine and/or sugar for a day, or slowly lower your intake over the course of a week. Notice how you feel without it.

SLEEP & STRESS

- Take a break from your day and take a walk.
- Avoid looking at your phone for at least an hour before you go to sleep tonight.
- Go to sleep an hour earlier than you normally do tonight.
- Clean your bedroom before going to sleep.
- Sign up for a meditation app on your phone and meditate for 15 minutes today.
- Set aside 10 minutes to stretch your muscles this evening. Stretch your big muscles first (i.e. hamstrings, arms, and back.)
- Go dancing.

‣ Enjoy a warm bath.

‣ Try the sauna or steam room at the gym. Take deep breaths while inside.

‣ Make a point to take five minutes away from your computer every hour. If you can't do that, take a longer, screen-free break from your day when you can.

‣ Smile! Set smile alerts on your phone to remind you to smile more (even if it's just at your computer monitor).

‣ Spend a few extra minutes grooming in the morning. You'll feel more confident when you walk out the door.

‣ Spend time with a pet. Consider adopting one or volunteering at a shelter, maybe even babysitting.

THE MENTAL PILLAR

GET TO KNOW OTHER PEOPLE

▸ Sign up to volunteer for a cause you care about.

▸ Write down the five people you hang out with most. Write down how you feel when you spend time with them. Write down what you learn.

▸ Make eye contact with someone in conversation today.

▸ When you ask someone how their day is, push for a deeper answer than "Good."

▸ Pay someone a compliment today.

▸ Ask someone you don't know well to lunch.

▸ Do something kind for a friend (or stranger) today.

▸ Practice deep listening. Instead of thinking of what you will say next in a conversation, make a point to listen closely to the other person and ask a follow-up question.

TRY NEW ACTIVITIES

▸ Go to a restaurant you've never been to or try out a recipe from a cuisine you don't often eat.

▸ Try a new activity, like rock climbing, kayaking, or golf.

▸ Join a meet-up group.

‣ Take a class to learn more about something you're interested in—such as pottery, painting, real estate investing.

‣ Exercise differently today. If you always go to the gym, exercise outside, try group exercise, or go on a bike ride. Switch up your routine.

EXPAND YOUR MIND

‣ Take a trip to the library and pick out a book from a genre you don't normally read.

‣ Instead of watching a movie this weekend, try a documentary.

‣ Listen to a podcast on your commute today instead of the radio.

‣ Join or start a book club.

‣ Dedicate 10 minutes today to reading news articles.

BUILD MENTAL STRENGTH

‣ Write down five things you want to focus on today. Set reminders for yourself throughout the day to continue focusing on them.

‣ When you find yourself feeling anger today, force yourself to laugh it off and smile. Attempt to bring positive thoughts back in.

‣ Do something that scares you today, even just a little.

‣ Set a reminder in your phone to spend five minutes in the morning cultivating a positive mindset. Spend that time writing down a positive quote, saying a positive affirmation, meditating, etc.

‣ Let go of a grudge today.

‣ Visualize achieving a written goal of yours. Take the first step to act on it.

‣ Say no to something that doesn't align with your values today. Start to practice saying no to things that don't make you feel good.

‣ Talk to yourself in the mirror and pay yourself a compliment.

‣ Pay attention to self-talk today. When you notice negative self-talk, replace it with how you would talk to a good friend instead.

‣ Seek out constructive feedback from a mentor, employer, etc.

‣ Make a list in the evening of three things you are grateful for that happened earlier in the day.

‣ Mark time on your calendar to do something that makes you happy tomorrow.

EMOTIONAL PILLAR

EMOTIONAL STRENGTH

▸ Before going to bed, journal about your day. Freewrite whatever comes to mind.

▸ Create a gratitude journal. Write down 3 things you are grateful for today. It could be as simple as life, health and happiness, a friendly smile, a promotion, etc.

▸ Spend time with someone whose positivity and energy you admire. Let it rub off on you.

▸ Press pause today. Take a conscious moment to "smell the roses."

▸ Pump yourself up in front of the mirror in the morning. Tell yourself that you've got it. You can handle everything on your to-do list that day.

▸ Practice four-square breathing for five minutes today. Take a deep inhale. Hold. Exhale slowly. Hold. Then repeat.

▸ Take a break from your day and do something physical. Go on a 10 minute walk or do some stretching.

▸ Practice forgiveness today. If someone cuts you off in traffic, grant them forgiveness. If you do something you regret, grant yourself forgiveness. Move forward from the experience.

▸ At a low point in your day, turn on your absolute favorite song and jam out for a few minutes.

▸ Take a technology break and go off the grid, even if only for a few hours.

EMOTIONAL INTELLIGENCE

▸ Try to imagine yourself in someone else's shoes. Think about what their day looks like: what time they wake up, what they eat, what they do for fun, what they worry about, etc.

▸ Go the whole day without saying something negative about someone else or judging them.

▸ Practice being more vulnerable today. Vulnerability increases intimacy; intimacy creates tighter relationships. Open up to someone you trust.

▸ Pay attention to your body language today and what you are saying without speaking.

▸ Identify and write down the top 5 positive emotions you feel today (e.g. joy, love, peace, happiness). Notice what triggered them.

▸ Identify and write down the top 5 negative emotions you feel today (e.g. frustration, angst, fear, annoyance). Notice what triggered them.

▸ Write down a list of your pet peeves. When you experience one, what do you feel? Then identify and write down the antidote to that feeling.

▸ Help someone else today. It can be as simple as holding open a door or picking up something they've dropped.

▸ Volunteer with a charity that helps people in your community.

▸ Approach someone that you don't know well and strike up a conversation.

RELATIONSHIP BUILDING

‣ Get coffee or go on a walk with a friend you haven't seen in a while.

‣ Call someone that you love just to chat.

‣ Pay a compliment to someone you value. Tell them what you value about them.

‣ Write down a positive emotion you'd like to be remembered for.

‣ When you think about texting a friend, opt to call them instead.

‣ Send a friend a postcard from your city or handwritten note to let them know you're thinking of them.

‣ Send a thank-you note acknowledging something kind someone did for you.

‣ Follow up with someone about something they told you the day before. Ask how their meeting went or how their child's school play went.

‣ When someone shares a negative emotion with you, avoid the impulse today to fix it or help them shake it off. Simply acknowledge their feelings and make sure they feel heard.

‣ Write down three people in your existing network you'd like to build stronger relationships with. Take the first step toward that goal in each relationship today.

SPIRITUAL PILLAR

PRAYER & CONNECTION

- Say a prayer. If you don't know what to say, say that.

- Make a point to practice humility today.

- Journal your prayer requests at night before bed.

- Give worship music a try.

- Notice and write down the small miracles you witness today (sun shining, birds chirping, a perfect cup of coffee, etc.)

- Try interchanging the word "lucky" with "blessed" today. What were you blessed to experience on this day?

- Find 10 minutes in your schedule to be still and quiet. Examine what you are most grateful for in that time. Examine what is lacking.

- Come up with a personal mantra to come back to in difficult moments. It can be a few words to help remind you how you would like to respond.

- Set an intention for your day. What kind of person do you want to be today?

- Get outside and spend time in nature today.

RELATIONSHIPS

- Start a conversation with someone you trust and admire about their faith. Practice opening up about your own.

- When confronted with someone who has different beliefs, try to understand why they believe that. Approach them without judgment.
- Ask a spiritual friend to hang out. Take the first step in surrounding yourself with people who make you better.
- When someone tells you something that is upsetting to them, pray for them.
- Forgive someone who has wronged you.
- Seek forgiveness from someone you have wronged.
- If you are strong in your faith, find an opportunity to mentor someone else.

SPIRITUAL KNOWLEDGE

- Take part in a small group or Bible study.
- Read a section of a religious text, like the Bible. Just start from the beginning.
- Try out a church. If you previously went but didn't connect to a certain church, try a new one.
- Start reading a faith-related book.
- Practice self-control and moderation by giving up something you enjoy today. If you're stuck for ideas, consider coffee, chocolate, sugar, or alcohol.
- If you come across a line of scripture or a spiritual quote, commit it to memory.

- Ask a spiritual friend if you can accompany them to church one week. Ask if they'll come to your church as well. Talk about the experience after.

- Sign up for a daily devotional.

- Ask someone you trust what their favorite prayer or scripture is.

PAYING IT FORWARD

- Encourage someone you know to practice gratitude. Draw attention to the good in their life.

- Donate your time or money to your church or a faith-based charity.

- Do five simple good deeds for others today.

- Put someone you love first today. Consider their feelings and hopes before your own.

PROFESSIONAL PILLAR

PROFESSIONAL DEVELOPMENT

‣ Write down your 1-year, 3-year and 5-year professional goals. Next, write down the steps you'll need to take to reach them.

‣ Make a point of showing respect to your colleagues and superiors today. Tell them you appreciate them.

‣ Examine your communication style. Would you feel comfortable if everyone in the company saw your emails? What impression do you give off? Spend time today examining how you could improve your communication to be more courteous and effective.

‣ Make a point of listening to your colleagues and mentors today. Don't focus your energy on impressing them. Rather, try to absorb their knowledge and ask questions.

‣ Brainstorm new ideas for your current company. Be proactive about pitching them and showing initiative.

‣ Maximize your online resume. Make sure that you are proud of any professional seeing your social media, including LinkedIn, Facebook, Twitter, and so on.

‣ Start compiling the positive feedback you receive at work into a folder. Refer to that folder when seeking a pay increase or more responsibility.

‣ Get dressed for success this morning. Wear an outfit that makes you feel confident.

▸ Find an industry newsletter to subscribe to for updates, information, and articles about your current industry or an industry of interest.

▸ Before bed, write down three things you hope to accomplish at work the following day. Practice looking forward to work, rather than dreading it, by getting ahead of your to-do list.

▸ Grab coffee with a colleague in a different department. Get to know what they do every day.

▸ Be the first person to show up for meetings today. Say hello and smile when colleagues come in the door.

▸ When you see someone producing great work or being a positive team player, recognize them for it. Let them know that you appreciate working with them.

FINANCIAL HEALTH

▸ Open a savings account for investing. Even if you don't have enough to invest yet, set a monthly goal to put into that account and research how you'd like to invest that money.

▸ Purchase a book on investing and start learning more about your options.

▸ Do the math today on how much money you would need to live on for 6–9 months without employment. Set a goal to start putting away money toward an emergency fund each month and make your initial deposit.

▸ Skip coffee or cocktails for a week. Deposit what you save into a savings account or use it to pay down a little extra debt. Don't keep it in your checking account to be spent on something else.

- If your company offers a 401k plan, enroll in it. If you're already enrolled, increase your contribution by 1%.
- Create a personal spending budget. Look for things you can cut back on to increase your saving or investing amounts.

EXPLORING NEW PROFESSIONAL PATHS

- Attend a networking event.
- Brainstorm new business ideas todays. If you have one, write the first page of a business plan for it. Take the first step to bring it to life.
- Ask someone you admire to coffee. Come prepared with a few thoughtful questions for them.
- Seek out an educational opportunity (ongoing education class, online course, etc.) that will help you improve professionally in one area. If it relates to your current job, explore whether the company will cover costs.
- Pick up a business book about something you find interesting (leadership, marketing, etc.).
- Start your day with a to-do list of all your professional tasks, including those related to side hustles, investments, and so on.
- Subscribe to a business or investing podcast. Listen to it while you commute today.
- Ask someone you trust to review your resume. Does it clearly and accurately portray the best you? If not, freshen it up.
- Start researching the real estate market in your area. Start in your current neighborhood and look up average rental rates, asking

prices, number of days on market. Start to get an idea of what it would take to purchase a rental property one day.

‣ Sit down with your calendar and find at least one hour per week (or per day if you can) to focus on other professional goals like starting a business, learning new skills, or reviewing your finances. When you find the time, block it off on your calendar and don't allow other things to be scheduled over it.

‣ If your college has an alumni group in town, sign up to hear about events. And go to them!

30 DAYS

APPENDIX B

OF CHANGE

NOW IT'S TIME FOR YOU to take control of your daily challenges! In Chapter 8, you set goals to help live out your values and mission statement. Here you can break those goals down into smaller challenges that can be accomplished in one day or you can experiment with new interests. It is up to you what you choose to challenge yourself with each day. Whatever you decide, write down your challenge below, along with the Pillar it most closely aligns with. Make sure you cover all 5 Pillars, even if they're not represented equally, and have fun with it!

Just remember the ultimate goal—to be better than you were the day before.

DAY 1

Date: .... Pillar: ....

DAY 2

Date: .... Pillar: ....

DAY 3

Date: .... Pillar: ....

DAY 4

Date: .... Pillar: ....

DAY 5

Date: .... Pillar: ....

DAY 6

Date: _____ Pillar: _____

_____

DAY 7

Date: _____ Pillar: _____

_____

DAY 8

Date: _____ Pillar: _____

_____

DAY 9

Date: _____ Pillar: _____

_____

DAY 10

Date: _____ Pillar: _____

_____

DAY 11

Date: _____ Pillar: _____

_____

DAY 12

Date: _____ Pillar: _____

_____

DAY 13

Date: _____ Pillar: _____

_____

DAY 14

Date: _____ Pillar: _____

_____

DAY 15

Date: _____ Pillar: _____

_____

DAY 16

Date: _____ Pillar: _____

DAY 17

Date: _____ Pillar: _____

DAY 18

Date: _____ Pillar: _____

DAY 19

Date: _____ Pillar: _____

DAY 20

Date: _____ Pillar: _____

DAY 21

Date: _____ Pillar: _____

_____

DAY 22

Date: _____ Pillar: _____

_____

DAY 23

Date: _____ Pillar: _____

_____

DAY 24

Date: _____ Pillar: _____

_____

DAY 25

Date: _____ Pillar: _____

_____

DAY 26

Date: _____ Pillar: _____

_____

DAY 27

Date: _____ Pillar: _____

_____

DAY 28

Date: _____ Pillar: _____

_____

DAY 29

Date: _____ Pillar: _____

_____

DAY 30

Date: _____ Pillar: _____

_____

ACKNOWLEDGMENTS

AS I THINK ABOUT all the amazing people in my life who I'd like to express my sincere gratitude and appreciation for in making this book possible, the list goes on. I truly believe success is never created alone. I am beyond blessed for my circle of family, friends, and colleagues for continually pushing me to new heights.

First, I would like to thank my wife, Joslyn. You have been instrumental in my, life and without you, I would not be the man I am today. Your support and encouragement in writing this book has made all the difference. Every day you make me want to be a better husband, father, friend, and man.

To my parents, Ahmed and Vicki, thank you for always being there for me, supporting me, and encouraging me to chase my dreams and be the best I can be. You've had a massive impact on the man I am today, and you were always there for me cheering me on every bit of the way.

To my brothers, Ramsey and Zak, and sister, Hanna, thank you for always pushing me, challenging me, and being there for me. Your encouragement and positive attitudes have continually helped push me to new heights. Thank you for being there for me not only as siblings but as best friends too.

To Jeff Saturday, thank you for your friendship, which has been invaluable. Your leadership in life and on the home front is admirable, truly living out what it means to live a Christian life. "As iron sharpens iron, so one person sharpens another." Thank you for sharpening me.

To Emilie Bingham, thank you for being so instrumental in bringing this book to life and making this all possible. I am forever grateful for the impact you have had on this process.

To all my friends near and far, thank you. I'm a firm believer that your network is your net worth in all Pillars of life, and I am grateful for the impact you have had on my life.

To all supporters of AlwaysSmilin and readers of my book, thank you. Life is an incredible journey, and we were born to blaze new trails and pioneer great adventures. Thank you for joining me on this incredible journey to positively impact the world.

And most of all, I thank God for guiding me, equipping me, and strengthening me.

ABOUT
AARON AMMAR

AARON IS AN ENTREPRENEUR, investor, author, and eternal optimist.

Born and raised in Texas, he founded his first business, a pressure washing company, while still in high school. He then moved to North Carolina to play Division I soccer at Appalachian State University, graduating with honors and earning degrees in Finance & Banking and Risk Management & Insurance.

Upon graduating, he held corporate roles at Travelers and XL Catlin and served as the Head of Risk Aggregation & Analytics at XL Catlin in the Enterprise Risk Management group. He cofounded and operates SPA Properties, a real estate business focused on providing affordable student and family housing, as well as The Ammar Team at Keller Williams Realty, helping clients buy, sell, and invest in homes.

Currently residing in West Hartford, Connecticut, he was a Partner at Y-Risk, an innovative insurance company focused on insuring the sharing and on-demand economy, recently acquired by The Hartford. He is also a Partner at Vixster, a waste and recycling company in North Carolina.

Aaron is passionate about business and startups and serves as an advisor to several companies. He is a performance coach through Performance Coach University, taught by world-renowned coach and speaker, Jairek Robbins.

He also serves as a board member for the Brantley Risk & Insurance Center at Appalachian State University and is active in the local Nutmeg Big Brothers Big Sisters program. Aaron enjoys spending time with his wife, Joslyn, son, Eli, and dog, Zane.

Made in the
USA
Columbia, SC